Portraits from
THE AMERICANS:
The Democratic Experience

with excerpts from the text and
a new introduction by
Daniel J. Boorstin

CAPTIONS
Rick Beard
Frederick S. Voss
Kenneth A. Yellis

PICTURE RESEARCH
Monroe H. Fabian
Marjorie Share

COORDINATOR OF EXHIBITIONS
Beverly Jones Cox

EXHIBITION DESIGNER
Joseph Michael Carrigan

Portraits from
THE AMERICANS:
The Democratic Experience

An exhibition at the National Portrait Gallery
based on Daniel J. Boorstin's
Pulitzer Prize-winning book

Random House *New York*

Copyright © 1975 by Smithsonian Institution
selections from *The Americans: The Democratic Experience* © 1973 by Daniel J. Boorstin

All rights reserved under International and Pan-American
Copyright Conventions. Published in the United States by
Random House, Inc., New York, and simultaneously in Canada
by Random House of Canada Limited, Toronto.

Library of Congress Cataloging in Publication Data

National Portrait Gallery, Washington, D.C.
Portraits from the Americans.

1. United States—Civilization—Exhibitions.
2. Portraits, American—Exhibitions. I. Boorstin,
Daniel Joseph, 1914-   The Americans: the democratic
experience. II. Title.
E169.1.N3745 1975   973'.074'0153   75-10269
ISBN 0-394-49896-8
ISBN 0-394-73105-0 pbk.

Manufactured in the United States of America

2 4 6 8 9 7 5 3

FIRST EDITION

PHOTO CREDITS:
Elton Schnellbacher, p. 5
Geoffrey Clements, p. 12
Duane Suter, p. 13
from Stefan Lorant's Lincoln: A Picture
Story of His Life, *p. 15*

Designed by Carole Lowenstein

ACKNOWLEDGMENTS

The assemblage of the portraits, photographs, and objects for this exhibition would not have been possible without the assistance extended by libraries, historical societies and museums, and corporation archives. The location of these pieces, many of them of a highly unusual nature, required extraordinary effort on the part of numerous individuals.

Special thanks are due Inez Calnek of the Equitable Life Assurance Society of the United States; David Lustig of the New England Mutual Life Insurance Company; Thomas Daly of Borden, Inc.; William King of the Duke University Archives; William Alex; The National Museum of History and Technology; Thomas Battle of the Moorland-Springarn Collection, Howard University; Roberta Gardner and Linda Zelevansky of Dun & Bradstreet, Inc.; Albert Tannler of the Joseph Regenstein Library, University of Chicago; Alan Perkins of the Drake Well Museum; Robert Lovett of Baker Library, Harvard University; Roderick Walker of Lincoln's Inn Library, London, England; Professor John Popplestone of the Archives of the History of American Psychology; Ruth Beasley of the Institute for Sex Research; Frank and William Gilbreth; Ernestine Gilbreth Carey; George Taylor of the Rockefeller Family Fund; and William A. Koelsch.

The Chicago Historical Society, the Art Institute of Chicago, the Newberry Library, the State Historical Society of Wisconsin, the Exxon Corporation, and The National Museum of History and Technology, Smithsonian Institution, rendered invaluable assistance.

We are also grateful to several individuals and organizations who spent time pursuing false leads we provided them. In many cases knowing where things weren't proved nearly as helpful as knowing where things were.

Lenders to the Exhibition

Baker Library, Harvard Business School
The Beinecke Rare Book and Manuscript
Library, Yale University
Borden, Inc.
University of California Library, Berkeley
Ernestine Gilbreth Carey
The Carnegie Foundation for the Advancement
of Teaching, New York City
The Chicago Historical Society
Clark University Archives, Worcester,
Massachusetts
The Concord Antiquarian Society, Concord,
Massachusetts
Detroit Historical Museum
Drake Well Museum, Titusville, Pennsylvania
Dun & Bradstreet, Inc.
Duke University Archives
Duke University
Equitable Life Assurance Society of the
United States
Exxon Corporation
Mr. and Mrs. Robert Frank Berliner
Incorporated Village of Garden City, New York
General Foods Corporation
Frank Gilbreth
Dr. and Mrs. Stephen P. Gill
Harvard Law School Library
The Rutherford B. Hayes Library, Fremont,
Ohio
The Misses Hollerith
Francis N. Iglehart
Illinois Historical Survey, University of Illinois
Library
Institute for Sex Research, Inc.,
Indiana University
International Harvester Company
International Museum of Photography,
Rochester, New York
The Johns Hopkins University
Porter Kier
Library of Congress
The Lilly Library, Indiana University,
Bloomington
The Honourable Society of Lincoln's Inn,
London

Arthur D. Little, Inc.
Eugenia Cassatt Madeira
Mary Wright McKee
Massachusetts Historical Society
Moorland-Spingarn Research Center, Howard
University, Washington, D.C.
Museum of the City of New York
The National Archives
National Cash Register Corporation
The National Museum of History and
Technology, Smithsonian Institution
University of Nebraska Library, Lincoln
New England Mutual Life Insurance
Company
The New Jersey Institute of Technology,
Newark
The New-York Historical Society
The Old Print Shop, New York City
Alfred Orendorff Collection
Otis Elevator Company
Piggly Wiggly Corporation
Parker Brothers
The Joseph Regenstein Library, University of
Chicago
Reis Library, Allegheny College, Meadville,
Pennsylvania
Rockefeller Family Archives
Sears, Roebuck and Co.
The Singer Company
Smithsonian Institution Libraries
Springfield City Library, Springfield,
Massachusetts
Stanford University Archives
Stanford Unviersity Museum of Art
The State Historical Society of Colorado
The State Historical Society of Wisconsin
Special Collections, Vassar College Library
Vassar College Art Gallery
Montgomery Ward & Co.
F. W. Woolworth Co.

FOREWORD

During these early years of its existence, the National Portrait Gallery has focused its attention mainly on political, military, artistic, and scientific personalities, and the historic episodes in which they played a part. This exhibition, based on Daniel J. Boorstin's Pulitzer Prize-winning *The Americans: The Democratic Experience,* offered an irresistible opportunity to introduce, through the medium of its brilliantly orchestrated format, a new cast of characters, most of whom we hope ultimately will be represented in our permanent collection.

To the roll of great American inventors, which includes such universally known names as Cyrus McCormick, Alexander Graham Bell, and Henry Ford (already in the Gallery), we now add figures like Jacob Perkins and John Gorrie, whose efforts resulted in the scarcely less significant prodigy of air conditioning. And we find not only the much-admired Frederick Law Olmsted, who taught us how to lay out our parks, but also Jesse C. Nichols, who gave us our first shopping center, an even more ubiquitous phenomenon in our national landscape.

Among the more famous faces are a couple of railroad lawyers whose better-known careers made very different tracks—Abraham Lincoln and Judah P. Benjamin.

Here, too, are Alexander Turney Stewart, the father of the department store; James Bogardus, whose development of cast-iron construction methods heralded both the skyscraper and the prefabricated building; and Clarence Saunders, whose notion of self-service led from the corner grocery to the chain-store colossi, victualers to the nation's growing population.

Included in the exhibition from our own century is child psychologist G. Stanley Hall, who is perhaps better known for having brought Freud to lecture in America; and Alfred Kinsey, whose *Sexual Behavior in the Human Male* took the plain wrapper off books of similar nature, not to mention the subject of sex itself. The husband-and-wife team of efficiency experts, Frank and Lillian Gilbreth, have made it from one kind of a picture show—*Cheaper by the Dozen*—to another in these historic halls. And few people are likely to know that the computerized age in which we live was programmed almost a century ago in the punch-card system developed by Herman Hollerith. The list goes on, and although many of the names on it—Borden and Birdseye, Swift and Armour—are household words in more ways than one, here we learn about the man behind the label.

Lest one mistake the picture developed in our exhibition as entirely one of sweetness and light, also shown are Ida Tarbell, who exposed the evils of Standard Oil, and, by implication, American business in general; Jacob Riis, who focused his camera on our slums; and Upton Sinclair, whose *The Jungle* revealed the abuses of the meat-packing industry. And if Claude McKay, Countée Cullen, and Langston Hughes sang in praise of the Harlem Renaissance, they still cried out against the vestiges of Middle Ages for the Black in America.

Along with the likenesses in Dr. Boorstin's gallery of "Go-Getters" are some of the objects, associated with their accomplishments, which help to complete the delineation of their portraits. These run the gamut from paper goods, like an eleven-page Lorenzo Delmonico menu of 1838, to patent models of Elias Howe's sewing machine—and Isaac Singer's, which turned the contraption right-side-up.

Here, then, is our composite portrait of the "Democratic Experience." And if there are those who still think you can't make a silk purse out of sows' ears, we even have one of those, made by none other than Arthur D. Little in 1921.

Marvin Sadik, Director

National Portrait Gallery
Smithsonian Institution

CONTENTS

PART II

INTRODUCTION
by Daniel J. Boorstin

This exhibit tells in ways more vivid and more direct the story which I have unfolded in *The Americans: The Democratic Experience.* Here are some of the people who, in the past century and a half, made countless, little-noticed revolutions, not in the halls of legislatures or on battlefields or on the barricades but in our homes and farms and factories and schools and stores, across the landscape and in the air, revolutions so little noticed because they touched Americans everywhere and every day. By their work not merely the continent but human experience itself, the very meaning of community, of time and space, of present and future, was revised again and again. These are the men and women whose ingenuity and rivalry, imagination and stick-to-it-iveness brought forth a newly democratic world: a nation aiming to bring everything to everybody.

These are a characteristically American kind of revolutionary. They have not been as celebrated as they deserve, precisely because their heroics were slow and usually hidden from public view—in the oil fields or the wheat fields, in inventors' attics or in lawyers' offices, in stockrooms and warehouses, at a printing press or in a laboratory, on the assembly line or in the darkroom. Their successes, while soon enough reaching the advertising columns, seldom were applauded in front-page headlines. Their names were not embalmed in the titles of treaties or epoch-making legislation. Their banner was the American Standard of Living.

While many consciously aimed to revolutionize our daily lives, others were thinking of something else—making a fortune, devising an outlandish contraption that would work, selling people a new product or finding a new way to sell old products cheaper and in larger quantities, playing with the wonderful world of numbers, exploring the foibles of human nature, devising a tasty new dish, or teaching people what they had never been taught before. These men and women were all collaborators toward a Great American Transformation—of how we traveled, how we talked to our friends or conducted our business, what we wore, or ate or read, where we lived, and how we raised and educated our children. It is hard to realize that for the most part this has all happened within little more than a century. The careers portrayed here reach into our own time.

While in *The Americans: The Democratic Experience* I translated the people and their works into words, in this exhibit we actually see the people and some of their works. The Old English proverb "Pictures are the books of the ignorant" could only have come from a snobbish age when books were the preserve of the rich and the learned. In our literate age, when printed matter is everywhere and everyone can read, when our newspapers and magazines and books are more and better illustrated with photographs than any earlier age could dream of, we are apt to forget the special virtues of the picture.

The picture has a depth and clarity and ambiguity not found in any historian's words. And these portraits tell us what the historian cannot. The historian in an arrogant metaphor sometimes claims to give us the "portrait" of an age, but he can give us only a translation. A translation of the look and feel and smell and sound into cold print. A translation of a three-dimensional multicolored changing past into two-dimensional black on white. He can never, so vividly as this, give us the self-portrait. In this exhibit we see the authentic portrait of the age, as painted or drawn or photographed by itself.

These portraits can remind us of what the historian, on purpose or unwittingly, tempts us to forget: that *they* were surprisingly like *us.* To bring these people out of the pages of books (where we have never met our friends or neighbors) into the range of our eyes is to bring them newly into our own community. However the costume may vary from frock coat to business suit, whether the subject has in hand a quill pen or a typewriter or a digital computer, the face always has a contemporary look.

In an age when we are mightily impressed by our ability to despoil or remake our environment, we do well to be reminded that man is the constant, that in him is our problem and our promise. This commonplaceness, this shocking familiarity of the human face tells us that a civilization must and can be read not only in its Great Works but in the faces of its unique individuals.

The historian is inclined to write about people wholesale. He generalizes about epochs and nations, he tells us about "the people." If he does not write broadly enough he leaves us dissatisfied, and we say that he has not made sense of the past. "A history-painter," said Sir Joshua Reynolds, "paints man in general." But the portrait-painter paints persons. He depicts life retail, which is the way we always experience it. The portrait-painter, Reynolds added from his copious experience, paints "a particular man, and consequently a defective model." Yet it is their very "defects" which make these persons interesting, and which made each of them like nobody else. From this exhibit we see why any label like "the Americans" is misleading, unless we remember that it is both plural and singular. No nation was ever built by "man in general." Where shall we read the individuality of men and women if not in their faces?

Another foible of historians is to separate men from their works. To focus our attention on the effects of "the cotton gin," "the railroad," "the automobile," or "the airplane" and treat the makers as if they were merely set designers and scene builders, memorable for their works and not for themselves. But the Go-Getters, the inventors, the merchandisers, and all the others we meet here, were not only producers of American civilization. They were also among its most characteristic products. What did their grand opportunities, their fortunes-won and fortunes-lost, their fantastic successes and abysmal failures—what did all these do to *them?* We can try to read this story in their faces.

A portrait-history is special, too, for the demands it does (and does not) make on the viewer. While each work of history is written in a particular language and for a particular audience, here in this exhibit is a kind of history which *everybody* can read. It is directed to all who know the human face, what it expresses, and what it tries to conceal. "A man of fifty," Edwin M. Stanton once observed, "is responsible for his face." Everybody's face is an involuntary autobiography.

Yet, what a face says is much less obvious than what is said by words. Each of us must decide from his own experience what this or that face means. This ambiguity, this intimate personal quality, is the peculiar challenge of portrait-history. If a book can be read, a face must always be deciphered, and each of us must use his very own key.

Of course there are styles in portrait-painting and in portrait-photography. The portrait can deceive as well as inform. Johns Hopkins or Henry Huntington can be given the stature of a Holy Roman emperor; John D. Rockefeller can be depicted as a childlike innocent; Upton Sinclair can be portrayed as a St. Francis-like lover of the race. Captains of industry can be retouched to look like Caesars, prophets, or at least like ministers of the gospel. But these ways of interpreting and misinterpreting, too, bring an authentic message from their age—and often from the very individual who is portrayed. Portraits, like books, can be bowdlerized, expurgated, and prettied-up. These acts of expurgation themselves tell us unashamedly what the age was afraid to see. The cosmetics of the portrait-painter can tell us what he had not the courage to say.

Your life and mine have been shaped by the men and women we see here. A full exhibition of *The Democratic Experience* would have to include the portraits of the millions of Americans whose lives have been transformed. Such an exhibition is beyond the scope even of this beautiful room (which in its day was reputedly the largest room in America). But the faces we see here can awaken us to an uncelebrated meaning of our democratized experience. It can awaken us to the range of human hopes and frustrations, of energies, ambitions, and courage which made possible the everyday miracles of our America.

xv

Portraits from
THE AMERICANS:
The Democratic Experience

MEN OF PROGRESS (from left to right): *Dr. William T. G. Morton, James Bogardus, Samuel Colt, Cyrus H. McCormick, Joseph Saxton, Charles Goodyear, Peter Cooper, Jordan L. Mott, Joseph Henry, Eliphalet Nott, John Ericsson, Frederick E. Sickels, Samuel F. B. Morse, Henry Burden, Richard M. Hoe, Erastus B. Bigelow, Isaiah Hennings, Thomas Blanchard, and Elias Howe.*
CHRISTIAN SCHUSSELE, OIL ON CANVAS, 1862, 51⅜″ × 76¾″
NATIONAL PORTRAIT GALLERY, SMITHSONIAN INSTITUTION

PART I
Everywhere Communities

Americans reached out to one another. A new civilization found new ways of holding men together—less and less by creed or belief, by tradition or by place, more and more by common effort and common experience, by the apparatus of daily life, by their ways of thinking about themselves. Americans were now held together less by their hopes than by their wants, by what they made and what they bought, and by how they learned about everything.

THE GO-GETTERS

The years when the continent was only partly explored were the halcyon days of the Go-Getters. They went in search of what others had never imagined was there to get. The Go-Getters made something out of nothing, they brought meat out of the desert, found oil in the rocks, and brought light to millions. They discovered new resources, and where there seemed to be none to be discovered, they invented new ways of profiting from others who were trying to invent and to discover. Lawyers, who in the Old World had been the staid props of tradition, became members of a Go-Getting profession, profiting from the hopes of others, from the successes and frustrations of boosters and transients.

Rounding Up Rock Oil

The new wealth that some Western Go-Getters found growing from the grass roots up on the cattle range had a counterpart in the discovery of a new kind of gold deep underground. But while the world of the cattle-

3

man and the cowboy enriched American folklore and folk song, the roundup of rock oil left few folk heroes. Still, the discovery of oil, the invention of new ways to bring it to the surface, the organizing of ways to collect and transport it and deliver it to market—all these matched the achievements of the more widely celebrated cattledom.

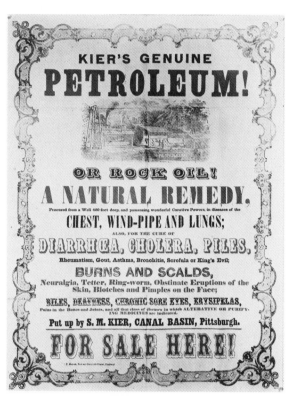

BOTTLE OF KIER'S "ROCK OIL REMEDY"

(left)
If Kier's claims were to be believed, fifty cents a pint was not too much to pay for his "healthful balm." "Cases that were pronounced hopeless," ran one advertisement, "and abandoned by Physicians of unquestioned celebrity, have been made to exclaim, 'This is the most wonderful remedy ever discovered.'"
PORTER KIER

ADVERTISEMENT FOR KIER'S "ROCK OIL REMEDY" 1852

(right)
When George Bissell spied the salt-well derrick in Kier's advertisements, in a New York drugstore in 1856, he was transfixed: here, finally, was the key to an improved method of oil recovery. If oil could be pumped from one of Kier's salt deposits as a by-product, the excited Bissell reasoned, why couldn't a similar well, properly drilled and located, be made to yield oil alone?
DRAKE WELL MUSEUM, TITUSVILLE, PENNSYLVANIA

SAMUEL M. KIER
1813–1874

Inhabitants of western Pennsylvania had known for years of the oil deposits lying beneath their farmlands; they saw little value in the thick, dark substance which periodically fouled the region's salt wells. The enterprising Samuel Kier knew better. Instead of cursing the "ugly grease" as it seeped into his salt well in the mid-1840's, he christened it the "Rock Oil Remedy" and began marketing it as nature's cure-all. Despite growing demand for his product, Kier's salt-well seepages yielded more "medicine" than he could sell. By the early 1850's he was refining his surplus for use in home lighting.

UNIDENTIFIED ARTIST, OIL ON CANVAS, CIRCA 1855, 34″ OVAL
MARY WRIGHT MCKEE

GEORGE H. BISSELL
1821–1884

Sitting in his New York law office in 1854 contemplating the future of his Pennsylvania Rock Oil Company, George Bissell had to admit that he knew very little about the potentials of the oil found on the company's western Pennsylvania farmlands. Nor could he escape the fact that there was still no economical way to recover this raw material. What he lacked in expertise, Bissell made up in determination and instinct. Within a year his intuition found the reinforcement it needed. According to the report commissioned from Yale scientist Benjamin Silliman, when properly refined his oil made an excellent illuminant; it could also be made to yield paraffin, all-weather lubricants, and a light-giving gas. All that remained now was to find an efficient method for extracting this versatile "black gold" from the ground.

REPRODUCED FROM A PHOTOGRAPHIC PRINT TIPPED INTO *The Early and Later History of Petroleum*, BY J. T. HENRY, PHILADELPHIA, 1873
SMITHSONIAN INSTITUTION LIBRARIES

SENECA OIL
COMPANY STOCK
CERTIFICATE

In 1858, oil leases held by Bissell's Pennsylvania Rock Oil Company were transferred to the Seneca Oil Company of New Haven, Connecticut. It was under the auspices of this second company that the search for an efficient means of extracting oil began. Judging from the pleasant scene which graced the stock certificates of the new enterprise, Bissell and his associates had little doubt that their venture would soon be prospering.
DRAKE WELL MUSEUM, TITUSVILLE, PENNSYLVANIA

DRAKE'S OIL RIG

(left)
Peter Wilson, Titusville druggist, and Edwin Drake, in silk hat, in front of the Drake oil rig
JOHN A. MATHER, PHOTOGRAPH, CIRCA 1859
DRAKE WELL MUSEUM, TITUSVILLE, PENNSYLVANIA

CONTRACT
BETWEEN S. M. KIER
AND E. L. DRAKE,
NOVEMBER 14, 1859

(right)
DRAKE WELL MUSEUM, TITUSVILLE, PENNSYLVANIA

EDWIN L. DRAKE
1819–1880

The task of developing a recovery method on Bissell's oil leases fell to Edwin Drake. A train conductor until neuralgia of the spine forced his early retirement, the frail-looking Drake seemed an unlikely choice for this formidable undertaking. Nevertheless, by April of 1859, after a year plagued by restless assistants and a chronic shortage of cash, his experiments with well-drilling began to show promise. By the following August he had succeeded in bringing in the country's first oil well with a yield capability of ten gallons a day. Strangely enough, while others made fortunes from his discovery, Drake did not. Much of his remaining life was spent in poverty.

JOHN A. MATHER, PHOTOGRAPH, 1861

DRAKE WELL MUSEUM, TITUSVILLE, PENNSYLVANIA

8

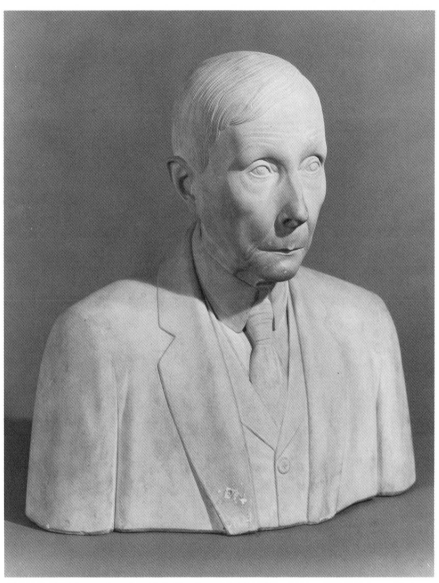

JOHN D.
ROCKEFELLER
1839–1937

Close to the Pennsylvania oil fields, from which tales of overnight fortunes filtered daily, the city of Cleveland by 1863 was already generously populated with proprietors of oil wells and refineries. The news that John D. Rockefeller was about to place a modest portion of his profits from his food-shipping firm in an oil refinery probably elicited no more than a passing remark from his fellow Clevelanders. Rockefeller, however, was no ordinary would-be oil baron. Methodical, precise, and diligent, he gave his venture an order and efficiency previously unknown in the industry. By 1870 his Standard Oil Company was the largest and most profitable refining enterprise in the city. A decade later it was the largest in the world and on its way to achieving almost total monopoly in American oil.

PAUL MANSHIP, PLASTER, NOT DATED, 21½″ HIGH
NATIONAL PORTRAIT GALLERY, SMITHSONIAN INSTITUTION

9

Generalized Go-Getters

It was no longer possible for a merchant to know personally all the men with whom he dealt. The systematic gathering and publication of reliable intelligence about businessmen itself became a field for the Go-Getters.

The relations between the more and the less developed areas of the world everywhere also provide a fertile field for lawyers. When there is a metropolis, a center of legislation and organization, a source of capital and knowledge and know-how which draws power and profit from lands at a great distance, there are all sorts of well-paid chores which require the lawyer's techniques.

The American West developed a relationship to the Atlantic-coast metropolises during the nineteenth century which was similar in many ways to that between British colonies, like Australia, and the metropolis of London. In Montana, Wyoming, Colorado, and the other states of the cattle-raising, mineral-rich West, the new investment capital had to be drawn from Eastern metropolises, thousands of miles distant. And this opened the way for enterprising lawyers who had novel duties and opportunities as promoters, organizers, and intelligence agents.

A new approach to legal education, signaling a vigorously American approach to the uses of law, was the invention of a dean of the Harvard Law School, Christopher Columbus Langdell. He had been selected in 1870 by Charles W. Eliot, the new president of Harvard, whose background as a chemist made him sympathetic to a new kind of laboratory approach to the law. By 1910 most American law schools had adopted the "case method." While the training of lawyers was given a new academic dignity, law students were rapidly given a wide and usable knowledge of practical legal situations. The law, once a metaphysic, had become a social science.

AN ENTRY FROM LEWIS TAPPAN'S DIARY, AUGUST 6, 1841

In establishing a credit-information service, Tappan thought he had hit upon a business that was fail-safe. "In prosperous times," he observed, subscribers "feel able to pay for information and in bad times they feel they must have it."
Initially, however, subscriptions to the Mercantile Agency did not come as easily as the comment implied. As his diary indicates, there were many days when Tappan's only solace was his deeply held religious faith.
LIBRARY OF CONGRESS

10

Engraved by J C Buttre

LEWIS TAPPAN
1788–1873

In 1840, with the silk-importing firm in which he and his brother were partners verging on collapse, Lewis Tappan was anxiously looking for a way to restore his fortunes. From his search he decided that the source of his troubles was his firm's unwitting extension of credit to poor risks. Spurred on by his own business needs, he set about establishing the nation's first credit-rating service. Known as The Mercantile Agency, the new venture with its network of agents and investigators at first raised dark suspicions, but by 1849, when Tappan retired to devote his full time to the abolition movement, his credit-rating service was on the way to becoming a fixture in American business life.

J. C. BUTTRE, ENGRAVING, PROBABLY AFTER A DAGUERREOTYPE OR EARLY
PHOTOGRAPH
NATIONAL PORTRAIT GALLERY, SMITHSONIAN INSTITUTION

JOHN M.
BRADSTREET
?–1863

Today the names Dun and Bradstreet are one and inseparable in the credit-rating business, but this was hardly the case a century ago. While Robert G. Dun was beginning his career in New York with The Mercantile Agency, John M. Bradstreet was in Cincinnati establishing his own credit-information firm. In entering the field, where until now The Mercantile Agency had dominated, Bradstreet proved himself an able competitor. By 1860 his printed semi-annual reports, containing conveniently keyed information on businessmen of practically every major city in the North and West, had aroused the admiration of even The Mercantile Agency. It was not long before the more experienced firm was adopting some of Bradstreet's techniques.

F. W. WRIGHT, OIL ON CANVAS, AFTER AN EARLY PHOTOGRAPH, 30″ × 25″
DUN & BRADSTREET, INC.

ROBERT GRAHAM
DUN
1826–1900

Before his retirement, Tappan had placed The Mercantile Agency on a sound footing; but it remained for Robert G. Dun to transform it into an international enterprise. Joining the firm in 1851, Dun played an important role in the Agency practically from the start. By 1859, when it took the name R. G. Dun & Company, he had become its sole proprietor. In assuming leadership, Dun instituted a vigorous program of expansion designed to keep pace with the nation's rapidly expanding industries and markets. By 1900, the year of Dun's death, R. G. Dun & Company had offices throughout the world.

BENJAMIN CONSTANT, OIL ON CANVAS, 1889, 45″ × 36″

FRANCIS N. IGLEHART

13

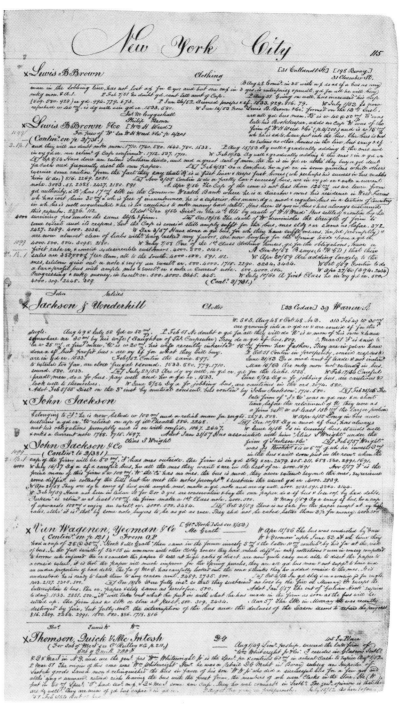

THE MERCANTILE
AGENCY'S NEW
YORK CITY REPORT
LEDGER OF THE
1850's

The Mercantile Agency's early reports on merchants investigated were recorded by hand in large ledgers. While generally the entries were confined to assets and business habits, they did from time to time touch on a subject's private life. In 1855, an agency subscriber seeking credit information on New York clothier Lewis Brown would have discovered that commercial success did not always preclude a taste for "fast" living and "fast horses."

BAKER LIBRARY, HARVARD BUSINESS SCHOOL

ABRAHAM LINCOLN
1809–1865

Abraham Lincoln exemplified the essential role of local attorneys in the operations of large-scale enterprises. Lincoln was retained by distant banks, insurance firms, gas companies, merchants, manufacturers, and most important, by railroads. He earned his largest fee, $5,000, in Illinois Central Railroad v. McLean County, *defeating the county's attempt to tax the railroad; in* Hurd v. Rock Island Bridge Company *he defended his client against the charge that the first trans-Mississippi railroad bridge—against which a steamboat had rammed, caught fire, and sunk—constituted a navigational hazard. Each suit's outcome ensured continued railroad expansion westward and sped the shift from water- to land-based transportation systems.*

A. M. BYERS, AMBROTYPE, MADE IN SPRINGFIELD, ILLINOIS, MAY 7, 1858
LOVE LIBRARY, UNIVERSITY OF NEBRASKA, LINCOLN

15

DECLARATION IN *ABRAHAM LINCOLN V. ILLINOIS CENTRAL RAILROAD*, 1857

Sparse settlement, light passenger and freight traffic, difficult terrain, primitive technology, and undercapitalization made the financial structure of most Western railroads precarious. Many would have tumbled into bankruptcy had the right of counties to tax them been upheld in Illinois Central Railroad v. McLean County, Illinois. *Lincoln emphasized the symbolic and practical importance of this victory and his role in winning it when he successfully sued for his $5,000 fee.*
ALFRED ORENDORFF COLLECTION

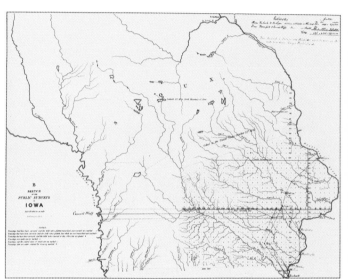

SKETCH OF PUBLIC
SURVEYS OF IOWA
SHOWING
BURLINGTON &
MISSOURI RIVER
RAILROAD ROUTE

(left)
*The secret of railroad penetration of the West was land, the only resource state
and federal governments had in sufficient abundance to supplement private
capital. Parallel rights of way, with their adjacent "sections," would often go to
rival railroads; each created its own market by selling land along its route to
settlers. The success of the Burlington & Missouri in Iowa largely resulted from
Joy's superior organization and staffing of its Land Department.*
MAP DRAWN BY D. MCCLELLAND
NATIONAL ARCHIVES

JAMES FREDERICK
JOY
1810–1896

(right)
*"In a country like the West," wrote James F. Joy, president of the Chicago,
Burlington, and Quincy Railroad Company, "it is impossible to remain
stationary." No one embodied that Western ideal of motion more completely than
Joy himself or did more to make that ideal a reality. From the 1840's through the
1870's, Joy pushed railroads deep into the West, consolidating, linking, and
strengthening weak and fragmented systems in Michigan, Illinois, Missouri, Iowa,
Nebraska, Kansas, and the Southwest. By negotiation, fund-raising, energy,
political maneuvering, resourcefulness, and sheer administrative ability, Joy
imposed order on a chaotic enterprise.*
"C. M. HAYES CO.," OIL ON CANVAS, DATE UNKNOWN, 30″ × 25″
DETROIT HISTORICAL MUSEUM

FROM A STAINED-GLASS WINDOW IN THE COLORADO STATE CAPITOL, DENVER

EDWARD OLIVER WOLCOTT
1848—1905

In the early 1870's, Edward O. Wolcott's restless quest for material success took him to booming Colorado, where his brother Henry was on his way to wealth and influence. A reputation earned in private law practice and as a prosecutor drew Ed Wolcott into conservative Republican politics. He twice engineered his own election to the United States Senate, where he spoke for silver-mining interests. His law firm thrived, meanwhile, as counsel for railroads and other corporations; Wolcott's expertise gave him a central role in major mining cases. The Wolcott brothers were invaluable for Eastern investors seeking guidance.

FROM A STAINED-GLASS WINDOW IN THE COLORADO STATE CAPITOL, DENVER

SAMUEL C. T. DODD
1836–1907

While Lewis Tappan demonstrated to businessmen the value of credit information, Samuel C. T. Dodd introduced them to a new form of organization, the corporate trust. Delegated by John D. Rockefeller in 1881 to bring legal order to Standard Oil's far-flung holdings, Dodd masterminded a reorganization that finally united Standard into an integrated whole. In doing this, he set a pattern which in the next two decades became a dominant trend in American industry. Despite a long career with Standard and invaluable service in subsequent reorganizations, Dodd never accepted Rockefeller's periodic offer to supplement his salary with company stock—an offer which if accepted would have made him a millionaire many times over.
EXXON CORPORATION

CHRISTOPHER
COLUMBUS
LANGDELL
1826–1906

A renowned "lawyers' lawyer" in New York, C. C. Langdell was summoned in 1870 to be law-school dean by Harvard's new president, Charles W. Eliot. During the twenty-five-year Langdell regime, the law school lengthened the course of study to two years and then three, broadened the curriculum, toughened standards for students and faculty and increased the numbers of both, expanded the library's collection tenfold, upgraded its physical plant, and in general acquired its present reputation and attracted imitators. Langdell transformed teaching law into a profession with techniques all its own. One of his most controversial innovations was the casebook method of teaching law. To Langdell, law was a science; the library was the laboratory where one discovered the first principles which govern all cases. The casebook method's utility, however, transcended Langdell's rationale; used only by Harvard until 1890, it spread rapidly thereafter and still dominates the teaching of law.

FREDERICK P. VINTON, OIL ON CANVAS, 1892, 50″ × 40″
HARVARD LAW SCHOOL

20

The Battles of the Inventors

The importance of any new technique in transforming American life could roughly be measured by the quantity of lawyerly energies which it called forth. While the inventor himself might be a lonely, unworldly genius, there was commonly somebody else nearby who saw the chance to make a fortune. These alert bystanders were often lawyers. There was hardly a major invention in the century after the Civil War which did not become a legal battlefield. While many battles were fought over patents, questions of patent law were inevitably confused with technicalities of contract, corporation law, taxation, and all sorts of common-law rights and duties. And these were entangled, too, with "interstate commerce," conflict of jurisdictions, and other mysteries of the Constitution.

The personalities were flamboyant, the hopes extravagant, the stakes enormous, and the products unprecedented. Of the many battles of the inventors, a few of the more spectacular were the battle of the sewing machine, the battle of the reaper, the battle of the telephone, the battle of the phonograph, and the battle of the automobile.

The Sewing Machine

In the middle of the nineteenth century, European travelers to the United States were struck by an American peculiarity. Just as travelers before them in the eighteenth century had noted the difficulty of distinguishing between American social classes by the habits of speech, and had noted that master and servant, even in the South, spoke in accents far more similar than did their English counterparts, they now noted the strange similarities of clothing.

In America it was far more difficult than in England to tell a man's social class by what he wore. Before the end of the nineteenth century, the American democracy of clothing would become still more astonishing to foreign eyes, for by then the mere wearing of clothes would be an instrument of community, a way of drawing immigrants into a new life. If, as the Old World proverb went, "Clothes make the man," the New World's new way of clothing would help make new men.

By the twentieth century, Americans would be the best-clothed, and perhaps the most homogeneously dressed, industrial nation. It is hard to imagine how it could have happened without the sewing machine. While the sewing machine had not been first conceived in America, the development of practical, widely salable machines for sewing was first accomplished here. It was the achievement of some remarkable American Go-Getters.

There was enough money in the sewing machine to enrich scores of inventors, would-be inventors, lawyers, promoters, salesmen, and businessmen. The two giants in the War of the Sewing Machine, which climaxed about 1850, were Elias Howe, Jr., and Isaac Merrit Singer. They battled not merely for money but for the honor of having been "the principal inventor" of the sewing machine.

21

1846 PATENT MODEL FOR ELIAS HOWE'S SEWING MACHINE

Elias Howe advanced sewing-machine technology by introducing the eye-pointed needle, moved by a vibrating arm, and a shuttle to produce an interlocking stitch. His patented machine, however, proved inconvenient to use. The cloth was held vertically by a set of pins to accommodate the horizontally positioned needle. Every few moments the cloth had to be removed and repinned to continue the seam.
DIVISION OF TEXTILES, THE NATIONAL MUSEUM OF HISTORY AND TECHNOLOGY, SMITHSONIAN INSTITUTION

ELIAS HOWE, JR.
1819–1867

A random remark promising its inventor a fortune led Elias Howe to develop and patent a sewing machine in 1845. His fortune, however, was slow in coming: a prohibitive price and widespread opposition from clothing manufacturers and seamstresses prevented him from selling a single machine.

Howe returned from England in 1849, where he had mistakenly hoped to profit from his invention, and discovered several manufacturers selling machines that clearly violated his patent. The impoverished Howe, with borrowed money, launched a five-year legal campaign that eventually brought him nearly $2 million and legal recognition as the primary inventor of the sewing machine.

UNIDENTIFIED ARTIST AFTER CHARLES LORING ELLIOTT, OIL ON CANVAS, DATE UNKNOWN, 50″ × 40″

DIVISION OF TEXTILES, THE NATIONAL MUSEUM OF HISTORY AND TECHNOLOGY, SMITHSONIAN INSTITUTION

ISAAC MERRIT
SINGER
1811–1875

"I don't care a damn for the invention. The dimes are what I am after." Whether Isaac Singer's invention—the first practical sewing machine—took only a flash of genius and eleven days' labor (as he later claimed) or a bit more time to develop, it produced profits almost immediately.

Patented in 1851, Singer's machine was in great demand because it could do continuous stitching, something Elias Howe's could not. By the time of Howe's patent victory in 1854, Singer's position in the sewing-machine industry was unassailable and his company's trademark was soon to become internationally known.

[EDWARD HARRISON?], OIL ON CANVAS, MAY 1869, 51⁵/₁₆″ × 38½″

THE SINGER COMPANY

24

ISAAC SINGER'S
PATENT MODEL
FOR
IMPROVEMENTS TO
HIS SEWING
MACHINE, 1855

Isaac Singer turned Elias Howe's sewing machine right-side-up. By placing the needle in a vertical position, he allowed for the continuous movement of the cloth, and thus permitted the machine's operator to sew a continuous seam. In all but his earliest models, Singer also introduced the foot treadle, which freed both of the operator's hands to handle the cloth being sewn.
DIVISION OF TEXTILES, THE NATIONAL MUSEUM OF HISTORY AND TECHNOLOGY, SMITHSONIAN INSTITUTION

The Reaper

American needs for new devices to explore and exploit the continent, and the random quest for fortunes, produced myriad new techniques, machines, and gadgets. It was a sign that the time was ripe for an invention when a number of inventors were perfecting it simultaneously, and when the best lawyers found it worth their while to organize the contending forces. The cast of characters in the American patent dramas varied, but the plot was remarkably uniform. Several men more or less simultaneously would devise a new machine or technique. Each wished to keep for himself or for his licensees all the profits of production. Meanwhile scores of businessmen would have entered the scene, having purchased fragments of the legal rights of the competing "original" inventors. Of course, every "improver" claimed that his version was the only one which really did the job. Legal battles went on for decades, but regardless of which inventor or businessman won a battle, the lawyers always won the war. Such was the case with the reaper.

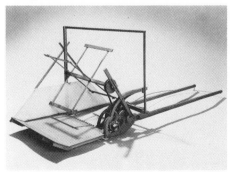

1831 MCCORMICK
REAPER,
REPRODUCTION
MODEL

At first McCormick tinkered rather than invented. He had a practical working reaper in 1831 and warned Obed Hussey of his intention to patent a grain harvester in 1833, but it was not until six months after Hussey filed that he followed through and gained a patent for an improved version of the machine shown here.
DIVISION OF AGRICULTURE AND MINING, THE NATIONAL MUSEUM OF HISTORY AND TECHNOLOGY, SMITHSONIAN INSTITUTION

CYRUS HALL MCCORMICK
1809–1884

At age twenty-two, Cyrus McCormick unexpectedly displayed genius, inventing a hillside plow and then a mechanical grain cutter, an idea that had long obsessed his father. With the failure of the family iron foundry, Cyrus turned his full attention to making and selling reapers. Annual improvements, discounts on outdated models, mass production, centralized parts manufacture, regional assembly, warranties, and easy credit, among other innovations, gave McCormick dominance of the booming industry he had created. Mechanization enabled the farmer to harvest all the grain he could plant, freed his sons to work in the city, and ensured cheap bread for millions of factory workers.

CHARLES LORING ELLIOTT, OIL ON CANVAS, DATE UNKNOWN, 20″ × 16″
NATIONAL PORTRAIT GALLERY, SMITHSONIAN INSTITUTION, GIFT OF CHAUNCEY
AND MARION DEERING MCCORMICK FOUNDATION AND MRS. GILBERT HARRISON

OBED HUSSEY
1792–1860

Obed Hussey had devised machines for grinding corn, crushing sugar cane, and making hooks and eyes, and was working on an improved candle mold when, in 1830, he turned to inventing a reaper. Moody and stubborn, Hussey worked alone, oblivious to other attempts to develop a practical machine to cut grain. His patent application antedated Cyrus McCormick's by six months, but differed from it materially. The twenty-five-year rivalry of McCormick and Hussey and the lapse of their patents spurred fierce competition and improved designs; success depended on advanced manufacturing and marketing techniques. Hussey's failure to adapt forced him to sell his factory in 1858.

FROM A LOST DAGUERREOTYPE, REPRODUCED IN *Obed Hussey Who, of All Men Made Bread Cheap,* BY FOLLETT L. GREENO, ROCHESTER, N.Y., 1912
LIBRARY OF CONGRESS

1847 PATENT
MODEL FOR
IMPROVED
CUTTING EDGE OF
THE HUSSEY
REAPER

As their basic patents neared expiration and were denied renewal, McCormick and Hussey sought to hold a large share of the expanding reaper market by design improvements which could be patented. The essential and most widely copied feature of Hussey's machine was its reciprocating saw-toothed cutting edge. The improved version, shown here, temporarily bolstered Hussey's deteriorating position in the industry.

DIVISION OF AGRICULTURE AND MINING, THE NATIONAL MUSEUM OF HISTORY AND TECHNOLOGY, SMITHSONIAN INSTITUTION

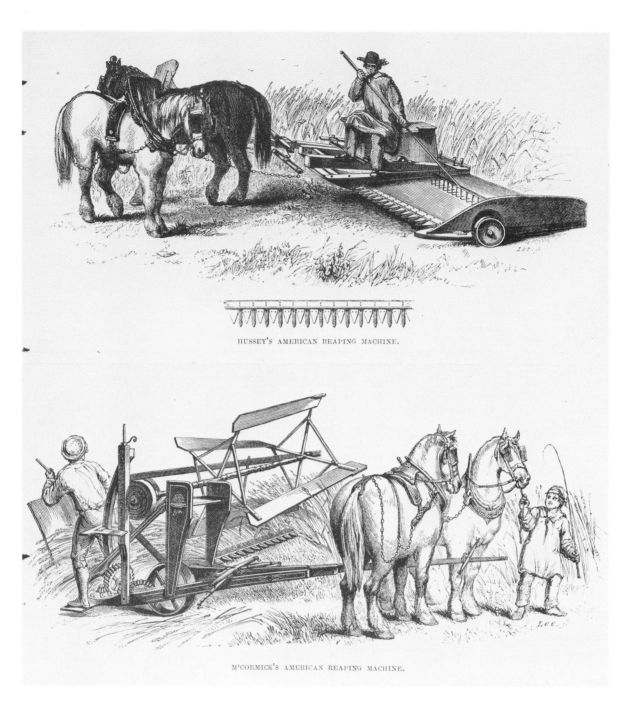

HUSSEY'S AMERICAN REAPING MACHINE.

M'CORMICK'S AMERICAN REAPING MACHINE.

THE MCCORMICK
AND HUSSEY
REAPERS

In the incessant competitive trials that Hussey demanded, the erratic performance of his and McCormick's reapers against each other and against rival machines obscured the importance of their differences in design. The saw-toothed blade near the ground made Hussey's machine a superior mower *to the higher straight-knife blade of McCormick's, but rendered it a less efficient* reaper. *Hussey's failure to exploit this factor and his refusal to adopt any refinements but his own lost him his market, and even he was forced to acknowledge defeat in 1858.*
ILLUSTRATED IN THE OFFICIAL CATALOG OF THE INTERNATIONAL EXHIBITION, LONDON, 1851
SMITHSONIAN INSTITUTION LIBRARIES

H. Ulke.

EDWIN MCMASTERS
STANTON
1814-1869

As reaper sales mounted, in 1854 McCormick instituted a patent-infringement suit against the John H. Manny Company. McCormick's competitors underwrote Manny's defense in an effort to break McCormick's hold on key features of reaper design. In McCormick's endless lawsuits, the nation's great legal talent participated on both sides. Already famous for his victorious prosecution of the Wheeling Bridge case, the scholarly Edwin M. Stanton enhanced his reputation further in McCormick v. Manny.

HENRY ULKE, OIL ON CANVAS, DATE UNKNOWN, 28½″ × 22½″
NATIONAL PORTRAIT GALLERY, SMITHSONIAN INSTITUTION

29

WILLIAM HENRY
SEWARD
1801–1872

With the stakes so high, McCormick paid to see another card; when John H. Manny and his backers won at the trial level, McCormick appealed. He retained William H. Seward, then senator from New York, who, like other congressmen, specialized in Supreme Court appearances. The lawyer-politician's shrewdness, and his ability to wax eloquent on the Constitution and the common law, commanded huge fees. But Seward failed to vindicate McCormick's claim to the Court; when asked to accomplish the same thing politically, he demurred on ethical grounds—and referred the request to his henchman Thurlow Weed.

GIOVANNI MARIA BENZONI, MARBLE, 1872, 28″ HIGH
NATIONAL PORTRAIT GALLERY, SMITHSONIAN INSTITUTION

30

JUDAH PHILIP BENJAMIN 1811–1884

By the 1870's, growing overseas reaper sales meant complex litigation over sales rights for the lawsuit-prone McCormick. When in 1878 he fired Otis S. Gage, his English representative, McCormick faced action from Gage and the firm to which Gage had assigned the English rights to sell the reaper without McCormick's approval. McCormick engaged Judah P. Benjamin, a former senator from Louisiana and member of the Confederate cabinet, who had escaped to England when the Confederacy collapsed and had begun a distinguished career at the English Bar. Benjamin's scholarly knowledge of both American and English law made him especially effective on appeals; he neatly extricated McCormick from the English legal maze by playing the manufacturer's adversaries off against each other.

FREDERICK PIERCY, ENGRAVING, 1883
THE HONOURABLE SOCIETY OF LINCOLN'S INN, LONDON

31

BELL'S AND GRAY'S
TUNED REEDS FOR
THE HARMONIC
TELEGRAPH

Alexander Graham Bell had not planned to invent the telephone. He hoped instead to improve the telegraph so that several messages could be sent simultaneously. Elisha Gray entertained the same hope and was able to file his own plan for a harmonic telegraph with the Patent Office two days before Bell did.

As the similarity between their tuned reeds shows, both men devised essentially the same system. The transmitter used a set of tuned reeds to send a current composed of several different frequencies, each carrying a separate message, over the same telegraph wire. Identically tuned reeds at the receiving end of the wire separated the current into its component messages.

DIVISION OF ELECTRICITY, THE NATIONAL MUSEUM OF HISTORY AND TECHNOLOGY, SMITHSONIAN INSTITUTION

The Telephone

When Bell's telephone was displayed at the Philadelphia Centennial Exposition in 1876, in the very year that Alexander Graham Bell had received his first telephone patent, it was still a great curiosity. Only two years later the first telephone appeared in the White House, under President Rutherford B. Hayes. Scores of inventors, including Thomas A. Edison and Emile Berliner, improved the telephone. By the early twentieth century the telephone had become an everyday convenience, and Bell's company, overtaking U. S. Steel, had grown to be the largest corporation in the United States.

On remote farms and ranches, medical care by telephone saved the life of many a child—and incidentally saved the doctor a long ride, in the days when doctors still commonly made house calls. New businesses were started by Go-Getters who sold their goods exclusively by telephone, having discovered that customers who had already formed the habit of throwing away their "junk mail" would still answer every ring. The telephone (like the typewriter, which was perfected at about the same time) provided a whole new category of jobs for women. By the time the fifty-millionth American telephone was ceremoniously placed on President Dwight D. Eisenhower's desk, it was unusual for any American family to be out of reach of the telephone.

ALEXANDER GRAHAM BELL
1847–1922

"My God, it talks!" exclaimed the Brazilian emperor while watching Alexander Graham Bell demonstrate his telephone at the 1876 Philadelphia Centennial Exposition. Soon the whole country was talking, for Bell's invention was immediately put to commercial use. His work, originally designed to improve the telegraph, produced a revolution in communication.

Such success brought imitators, most notably the Western Union Company, and Bell was soon embroiled in seemingly endless patent litigation. His patent, however, withstood all assaults—testimony to his inventive insight. The creation of the telephone has often overshadowed Bell's research on deafness, a work he considered more important.

MOSES WAINER DYKAAR, MARBLE, 1922, 24¾″ HIGH

NATIONAL PORTRAIT GALLERY, SMITHSONIAN INSTITUTION, GIFT OF
DAVID F. DYKAAR

ELISHA GRAY
1835–1901

A few hours meant the difference between fame and relative anonymity for Elisha Gray. Later on the very day when Alexander Graham Bell filed a patent application for his telephone, Gray filed a caveat, or report of an invention not yet perfected. The subsequent formation of Bell Telephone Company as a competitor led Western Union to buy the telephone patents of both Gray and Thomas Edison and wage an ultimately unsuccessful infringement battle.

Gray never recovered from his disappointment, though he acquired about seventy patents for his electrical inventions such as the telautograph, a device that transmitted facsimile writing and drawing.

NATIONAL CASH REGISTER CORPORATION

The Phonograph

Few important modern inventions were as much the work of one man as the phonograph was Thomas Edison's. Though he was trying to make widespread use of the telephone possible despite its high cost, Edison's earthshaking first recorded message—the words to "Mary Had a Little Lamb"—presaged the enormous entertainment potential of his invention. But Edison, partially deaf and nonmusical, waited more than a decade before he sought to exploit the market for home music machines.

Genius that he was, Edison could not think of everything. Emile Berliner's gramophone was superior in every respect to Edison's phonograph: the turntable-and-disc method produced truer sound, greater economy, and easier reproducibility than Edison's cylindrical design. After Berliner's breakthroughs, preserving the musical moment became routine. By the last third of the twentieth century, it was Mozart for the millions and the Beatles for the billions.

34

THOMAS EDISON'S
TIN-FOIL
PHONOGRAPH,
CIRCA 1878

Thomas Edison's phonograph both recorded and reproduced sounds. A grooved cylinder covered with tin foil was turned by hand against a stationary needle attached to two diaphragms. Speaking into one of the diaphragms caused the needle to vibrate and so left grooves of varying depth on the tin foil. When the diaphragms were readjusted and the cylinder rewound and turned against the needle again, the grooves reproduced the original sounds.
DIVISION OF MECHANICAL AND CIVIL ENGINEERING, THE NATIONAL MUSEUM OF HISTORY AND TECHNOLOGY, SMITHSONIAN INSTITUTION

THOMAS ALVA
EDISON
1847–1931

"Everybody was astonished. I was always afraid of things that worked the first time." This candid remark, made with reference to the invention of the phonograph, characterized Thomas Edison's trial-and-error approach to his work. Edison and his colleagues at Menlo Park eventually held nearly two thousand patents.

Edison viewed invention as a social duty, and he did not consider an invention successful until it was commercially feasible. The phonograph languished for ten years after its creation, because Edison saw no mercantile potential in it. Many of his other inventions, such as the light bulb and the motion-picture camera, were more readily mass-marketed.
ABRAHAM A. ALEXANDER, OIL ON CANVAS, CIRCA 1889, 44¾″ × 54½″
NATIONAL PORTRAIT GALLERY, SMITHSONIAN INSTITUTION

EMILE BERLINER
1851–1929

(left)
Emile Berliner drastically improved earlier inventions of both Alexander Graham Bell and Thomas Edison. In 1877 Berliner patented the carbon microphone transmitter, the basis for all telephone transmitters. Bell's original telephone had used the same instrument for both speaking and listening.

    Ten years later Berliner patented the gramophone. To record sounds, his invention used a flat disk rather than the cylinder utilized by Edison's phonograph. These disks were reproduced from a master disk and were made of a durable shellac compound. The credit for first recording sound remains Edison's; the credit for devising the convenient, easily stored platter-record should be Berliner's.

H. WILLARD ORTLIP, OIL ON CANVAS, DATE UNKNOWN, 29½″ × 24″
MR. AND MRS. ROBERT BERLINER FRANK

EMILE BERLINER'S
1888 GRAMOPHONE

(right)
The improvements Emile Berliner incorporated in his gramophone made it the basis for the phonograph industry. His disk reproduced sound by varying the width of the grooves rather than their depth, as did Edison's cylinder. A mobile needle was propelled along the grooves by rotating the disk on a turntable very much like those in use today.

DIVISION OF MECHANICAL AND CIVIL ENGINEERING, THE NATIONAL MUSEUM OF HISTORY AND TECHNOLOGY, SMITHSONIAN INSTITUTION

SELDEN PATENT MODEL, 1895

(left)
In 1879 George Baldwin Selden submitted a patent model and general description of a "road engine." Unable to find financial backers, he made additions and improvements until his patent was granted November 5, 1895. Despite advances in automotive technology, Selden's patent seemed so unassailable that the major companies formed the Association of Licensed Automobile Manufacturers to purchase the right to its use in exchange for a royalty of 1¹/₄ percent of each car's retail price.
DIVISION OF TRANSPORTATION, THE NATIONAL MUSEUM OF HISTORY AND TECHNOLOGY, SMITHSONIAN INSTITUTION

UNUSED PATENT PLATE

(right)
DIVISION OF TRANSPORTATION, THE NATIONAL MUSEUM OF HISTORY AND TECHNOLOGY, SMITHSONIAN INSTITUTION

The Automobile

None of the legal battles was more prolonged, or more dramatic, than the Battle of the Automobile. While Henry Ford's name became a household word and he became an American folk hero, his main opponent, George Baldwin Selden, remained obscure to history, even though his skillful combination of mechanical know-how and legal technique dominated the production of automobiles in the early, formative years of the industry.

The long legal battle, which began in 1903 and lasted over eight years, was to be a victory for the lawyers on both sides. The total amount paid in royalties under the Selden claim was about $5.8 million. But after subtracting all the various fees and commissions for production, management, sales, and legal advice, the sum that actually trickled through the numerous corporate and partnership agreements into Selden's own pocket was only about $200,000. Lawyers' fees on Selden's side in the first three years of the litigation against Ford came to $225,000, and were matched by a similar sum in the next five years. Ford paid his lawyers about $250,000.

GEORGE BALDWIN
SELDEN
1846–1922

"Morally the victory is mine," said George Baldwin Selden, but the 1911 court decision that broke his monopoly over the American automobile industry was a Pyrrhic victory. In 1879 Selden had made first application for a patent describing only the general features of his automobile. The patent, which assured Selden a royalty on every car produced in the United States, was not granted until 1895, however, by which time the auto industry had become lucrative.

*   Henry Ford's refusal to pay these royalties set off an eight-year court battle that finally held Selden's patent valid but denied that Ford and the other manufacturers were infringing on it.*

THE ROCHESTER MUSEUM AND SCIENCE CENTER

HENRY FORD
1863-1947

"No man on earth was entitled to any 'rake-off' from that particular car," Henry Ford remarked after his victory in the Selden patent case. The court decision of 1911 enhanced Ford's reputation and marked his rise to preeminence among American automobile manufacturers.

His industrial success rested in large part on his introduction and refinement of the assembly-line technique, which by 1925 produced a new car every ten seconds of the working day. His methods revolutionized industrial production around the world.

H. WOLLNER, BRONZE, 1963 CASTING AFTER 1937 PLASTER, 16½″ HIGH
NATIONAL PORTRAIT GALLERY, SMITHSONIAN INSTITUTION, GIFT OF THE HENRY
FORD TRADE SCHOOL ALUMNI ASSOCIATION

39

HENRY FORD IN HIS FIRST AUTOMOBILE, THE 1896 QUADRICYCLE

GEORGE BALDWIN SELDEN AND HIS SON WITH A SELDEN BUGGY

The court decision that broke Selden's hold on the American automobile industry turned on the distinction between a two- and a four-cycle engine. During the 1870's Selden had developed a light three-cylinder model of the Brayton two-cycle engine. Over the following two decades, advances in automotive technology produced the more efficient Otto four-cycle engine, the one used by Ford and other manufacturers. The technical differences between the two engines were the basis for the ruling that Ford was not violating Selden's patent rights. Although dated "1877," Selden's car was built much later, with most of the engine parts made after 1904.

40

STEWART'S CAST
IRON PALACE

Alexander Turney Stewart's ever-expanding dry-goods business demanded ever larger stores. In 1862 he opened the largest of these, a five-story cast-iron and stone building that covered an entire city block. The Cast Iron Palace cost $2.75 million and was serviced by two thousand employees. It stood until a spectacular fire destroyed all but the frame in 1956.
PHOTOGRAPH MADE BY THE DETROIT PHOTOGRAPHIC CO., 1903
LIBRARY OF CONGRESS

BUILDERS OF CONSUMPTION COMMUNITIES

Invisible new communities were created and preserved by how and what men consumed. As never before, people used similar, and similarly branded, objects. The fellowship of skill was displaced by the democracy of cash. No American transformation was more remarkable than these new American ways of changing things from objects of possession and envy into vehicles of community. Nearly all objects, from the hats and suits and shoes men wore to the food they ate, became symbols and instruments of novel communities. Now men were affiliated less by what they believed than by what they consumed. The unique object, except for jewels and works of art, was an oddity and became suspect. If an object of the same design and brand was widely used by many others, this seemed an assurance of its value.

Consumers' Palaces

Between the Civil War and the beginning of the new century there appeared grand and impressive edifices—Palaces of Consumption—in the principal cities of the nation and in the upstart cities that hoped to become great metropolises. A. T. Stewart's, Lord & Taylor, Arnold Constable, R. H. Macy's in New York City; John Wanamaker in Philadelphia; Jordan Marsh in Boston; Field, Leiter & Co. (later Marshall Field & Co.) and the Fair in Chicago. And even smaller cities had their impressive consumers' palaces—Lazarus in Columbus, Ohio, and Hudson's in Detroit, among others.

"Department store" was an Americanism in general use before the opening of the twentieth century. This institution, which became so widespread that it was hard for Americans to believe that it had not always existed, was a large retail shop, centrally located in a city, doing a big volume of business, and offering a wide range of merchandise including clothing for women and children, small household wares, and usually dry goods and home furnishings. While not invented in the United States (there were a few pioneer examples in Paris), it flourished here as nowhere else. These grand new consumers' palaces were to the old small and intimate shops what the grand new American hotels were to the Old World inns. Like the hotels, the department stores were symbols of faith in the future of growing communities. For citizens of the sprouting towns, the new department-store grandeur gave dignity, importance, publicity, and even glamour to the acts of shopping and buying—newly communal acts in a new America.

ALEXANDER
TURNEY STEWART
1803–1876

"Not one of them has his discretion. They are simply machines working in a system that determines all their actions." Alexander Turney Stewart's system produced a dry-goods empire of several stores in Europe as well as New York's Cast Iron Palace, then the world's largest retail store. Unlike smaller retail shops, his pioneer department store allowed little independence or initiative to the individual clerk.

Stewart owed his $40 million fortune to his merchandising innovations. His stores were among the first to be departmentalized, to allow customers to browse unaccompanied by a clerk, to eliminate bargaining by setting a fixed price, and to permit the return of merchandise.

DETAIL FROM T. P. ROSSITER, OIL ON CANVAS, CIRCA 1865, 30″ × 25″
INCORPORATED VILLAGE OF GARDEN CITY, NEW YORK

42

REPRESENTATION
OF THE FIRST CAST
IRON HOUSE
ERECTED
INVENTED BY
JAMES BOGARDUS

*The completion in 1849 of his own factory, the Eccentric Mill Works, ably
demonstrated the convenience of James Bogardus' innovative building system.
Assembled on the site (at Centre and Duane streets) from prefabricated cast-iron
elements, the factory took but a few weeks to complete. In 1859 it was
disassembled just as quickly when street widening necessitated clearing the site.*
LITHOGRAPH, PUBLISHED BY ACKERMAN, NEW YORK, CIRCA 1850
MUSEUM OF THE CITY OF NEW YORK

JAMES BOGARDUS
1800–1874

*In 1848 James Bogardus constructed a new factory in New York, which used cast
iron for the floors, frames, and building supports for the first time. To a generation
whose buildings seldom exceeded five or six stories in height, the advantages of cast
iron over masonry soon became obvious. It was lighter, allowed for more windows,
and could be speedily assembled or disassembled.*

    *Bogardus (second from the left), already a noted inventor, patented his
method of assembly and was soon engaged in constructing several cast-iron business
buildings. One of the more famous of these was the Cast Iron Palace, completed
for dry-goods millionaire Alexander Turney Stewart in 1862.*
DETAIL FROM CHRISTIAN SCHUSSELE'S PAINTING *Men of Progress,* 1862,
51⅜″ × 76¾″

NATIONAL PORTRAIT GALLERY, SMITHSONIAN INSTITUTION

ELISHA GRAVES
OTIS
1811–1861

*When Elisha Graves Otis was directing the erection of a new factory which
required an elevator, he proceeded to devise one with unique features. He used
pulleys instead of counterweights; should the rope fail with the added strain, the
cage would be held firmly in place by a ratchet safety device. Otis dramatically
demonstrated his advance at the New York Crystal Palace Exposition in 1854,
cutting the rope with himself inside the cage. Otis' invention of a safe and rapid
passenger elevator gave impetus to the modern department store; by building
vertically, merchants could locate large stores in densely populated areas despite
high real estate costs.*
UNIDENTIFIED ARTIST, ENGRAVING, DATE UNKNOWN
NATIONAL PORTRAIT GALLERY, SMITHSONIAN INSTITUTION

THE NEW YORK
CRYSTAL PALACE

Here Otis first sold the public on his safety elevator.
F. F. PALMER, LITHOGRAPH, PUBLISHED BY NATHANAEL CURRIER, 1853
MUSEUM OF THE CITY OF NEW YORK, J. CLARENCE DAVIES COLLECTION

ROWLAND HUSSEY
MACY
1822–1877

(left)
A career that included a four-year whaling voyage and two years in Gold Rush San Francisco left R. H. Macy with few prospects at age thirty-six. But Macy's ideas, failures elsewhere, found their time and place in New York of the 1860's, where his small fancy dry-goods shop grew into one of the great early department stores. A Quaker, Macy adhered to the "true value" principle, fixing his prices as low as possible. He used newspapers extensively and anticipated modern advertising techniques to bring in customers from the whole New York metropolitan region, to whom he offered the total range of goods they desired at attractive prices.
GEORGE E. PERINE, ENGRAVING, DATE UNKNOWN
NATIONAL PORTRAIT GALLERY, SMITHSONIAN INSTITUTION

R. H. MACY'S FIRST
STORE, AT
FOURTEENTH
STREET AND SIXTH
AVENUE, NEW
YORK, CIRCA 1869

(right)
In 1858 Macy opened his Fourteenth Street store with a small stock of "fancy goods," little money, and boundless optimism. Thanks to low fixed prices, quality merchandise bought and sold for cash, vigorous and creative advertising, and an able staff which included women in important positions, Macy's original store soon absorbed its neighbors.
DIVISION OF COSTUME AND FURNISHINGS, THE NATIONAL MUSEUM OF HISTORY AND TECHNOLOGY, SMITHSONIAN INSTITUTION

Nationwide Customers

Chain Stores

Just as department stores drew together thousands within the city in their consumers' palaces, other new enterprises reached out from city to city, creating nationwide consumption communities. Chain stores, pioneers of the everywhere community, built communities of consumers across the land. The expression "chain store," an Americanism firmly settled into the language by the beginning of the twentieth century, described one of a group of similar stores under common ownership. Although, like the department store, the chain store was not an American invention, here it too became a newly powerful institution.

GEORGE
HUNTINGTON
HARTFORD
1833–1917

George Huntington Hartford resembled P. T. Barnum, combining business sense with a talent for flamboyant publicity. His idea was to cut the cost of tea to the New York consumer from a dollar to thirty cents a pound by eliminating the middlemen; in 1859 he formed The Great American Tea Company to do just that. Hartford extended his idea to other goods as well, while enticing customers with brightly lit façades, pagoda-shaped cashiers' cages, and premiums. The Great Atlantic and Pacific Tea Company superseded Hartford's original firm in 1869, spreading nationwide. Hartford's two sons introduced innovations, such as the cash-and-carry "economy stores" in 1912, which made A & P the world's largest food-marketing network.
IVAN G. OLINSKY, OIL ON CANVAS, DATE UNKNOWN, 36″ × 30″
GREAT ATLANTIC & PACIFIC TEA COMPANY, INC.

WOOLWORTH'S
LANCASTER,
PENNSYLVANIA,
STORE

(left)
This was F. W. Woolworth's first successful five-and-ten, as it appeared in about 1885.
LANCASTER COUNTY HISTORICAL SOCIETY, LANCASTER, PENNSYLVANIA

A SIGN FROM AN
EARLY
WOOLWORTH
STORE

(right)
Woolworth discovered early that an appealing sign announcing an even more appealing price did not necessarily guarantee buyers for his goods. The colorful display of merchandise was just as important. "To push trade in dull season," he urged his store managers in 1888, "keep your goods in attractive shape as possible and trim your windows twice a week..."
F. W. WOOLWORTH COMPANY

Five-and-Ten

New classes of merchandise came into being, characterized not by their quality or function, but by their *price*. One of the most spectacular careers in American history and some of the nation's most distinctive institutions were built on this simple new notion. The department store was a consumers' palace; the five-and-ten was a consumers' bazaar. Both were places of awakening desire. The department store displayed items of all prices and shapes and sizes and qualities; and the five-and-ten displayed a tempting array of items which one could buy for the smallest units of cash. If an attractive item was offered at a low enough price, the customer would buy it if he needed it—but if the price was low enough and in convenient coin, perhaps the customer would buy it anyway on the spur of the moment, whether or not he "needed" it. In a world where the fixed price and the public price were only beginning to be known, where haggling was still a social pastime, it required a bold imagination to conceive the five-and-ten way of merchandising.

FRANK W.
WOOLWORTH
1852–1919

When Frank Woolworth struck out on his own in 1879, it was to found a store chain exclusively devoted to merchandise selling at ten cents or less. The idea of assembling and marketing items at a price of five or ten cents was not new, but generally it was regarded as a somewhat underhanded trick for luring customers into a store to buy the establishment's more expensive goods. Woolworth's attention-getting displays and resourceful wholesale buying soon convinced the public otherwise. By 1910 the red-and-gold sign announcing the presence of Woolworth's Five-and-Ten was a sight familiar to shoppers throughout the nation.
J. J. CADE, ENGRAVING CIRCA 1910
NATIONAL PORTRAIT GALLERY, SMITHSONIAN INSTITUTION

Self-Service

A novel merchandising plan for forcibly exposing a customer to the storekeeper's whole stock came to be called, somewhat euphemistically, "self-service." While this popular term emphasized the absence of a salesman, the revolutionary significance of the invention was that by making the goods "sell themselves," it established a new relation between each buyer and everything offered for sale. In stores of this type the attendant was needed to service the goods, not the customer. The "customer" had been transformed from a willing consumer with specific demands into an unwitting target of the seller's packaging and display. This transformation was produced by the new architecture and technology of distribution. From the humble beginnings of a small "Piggly Wiggly" which admitted customers like piglets through turnstiles, channeling them back and forth through a maze which required them to follow a prescribed path, the "self-service" store grew into the vast "supermarket." By the 1930's, "supermarket" had entered the language to describe a store which combined self-service, cash-and-carry, and a vast assortment of goods. By about 1950 the trade defined a supermarket as such a store with an annual volume of at least a half-million dollars.

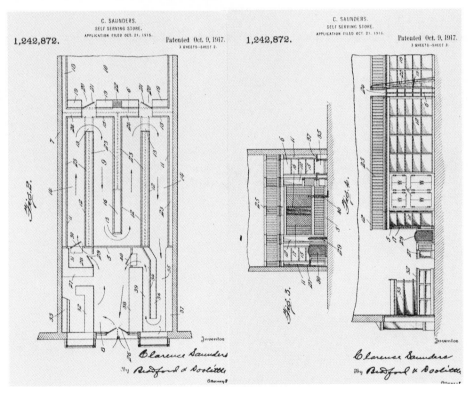

PLAN AND ELEVATION OF SAUNDERS' "SELF-SERVING" STORE

Clarence Saunders' floor plan, reproduced here from the 1917 Patent Office pamphlet, ingeniously exposed the customer to all of the store's merchandise. Admitted through a turnstile, the shopper was channeled along aisles lined with shelves displaying the goods. The customer selected his purchases and took them to the check-out counter, the store's only exit. This self-service system lowered the costs of operating the store and so helped to lower prices.
PIGGLY WIGGLY CORPORATION

CLARENCE
SAUNDERS
1881-1953

*During 1916, Clarence Saunders revolutionized the corner grocery by introducing
the nation to the first self-service food store. His idea was immediately popular, for
the low overhead produced generous profits, and by 1922 Saunders owned or
franchised more than twelve hundred Piggly Wiggly Stores.*

*Unsuccessful stock market machinations bankrupted Saunders, however, and
forced him to sever his ties with Piggly Wiggly. He soon launched a second
successful grocery chain with the unlikely name of Clarence Saunders, Sole Owner
of My Name, Stores, Inc., only to be ruined by the Depression. Undaunted, the
grocer spent the rest of his life trying to perfect Keedoozle, his idea for an
electrically operated grocery store.*
PIGGLY WIGGLY CORPORATION

Mass Periodicals

Technological advances in printing and typesetting, as well as the growth of cities, brought into being mass-circulation newspapers and magazines. Large-scale merchandising—the rise of the department store, mail-order houses, and chain stores—created a need for large-scale advertising. By sensational news and features—exposés, crimes, comic strips, sports news, and manufactured events—the mass-circulating newspapers attracted a large readership to justify their costs and satisfy their advertisers.

IDA TARBELL
1857-1944

By 1900 the call to investigate, expose, and reform was a dominant trend in American journalism, and it was no surprise when S. S. McClure, publisher of McClure's, asked staff writer Ida Tarbell to begin work on a series of investigative articles on the great Standard Oil monopoly. The methodically researched result and the response it generated did, however, come as a surprise. As each installment brought new disclosures of the cold-blooded, at times brutal, practices employed by this industrial leviathan against competitors, reader indignation mounted. By the end of the series, Standard had become the symbol of all that was wrong with American business. As for the woman responsible for this uproar, she was being hailed as a modern Joan of Arc.
CECILIA BEAUX, PENCIL SKETCH, CIRCA 1920, 22½″ × 17¾″
REIS LIBRARY, ALLEGHENY COLLEGE, MEADVILLE, PENNSYLVANIA

51

NELLIE BLY
(ELIZABETH
COCHRANE)
1867–1922

In filling the public appetite for the sensational, few were more adept than Nellie Bly, reporter for the New York World. *Born Elizabeth Cochrane, the petite Miss Bly joined the paper in 1888 where her first assignment involved being committed to an insane asylum. Soon the* World's *readers were engrossed in an electrifying account of the sordid conditions seen and suffered during her ten-day confinement. A year later the* World *announced that reporter Bly would prove that the globe-circling record set by Phileas Fogg in Jules Verne's* Around the World in Eighty Days *did, indeed, have basis in "ACTUAL FACT." For days, news of her whirlwind progress from country to country held readers in thrall. Finally, stopwatch in hand and bands blaring, she was back at her starting point in New York. Her time: 72 days, 6 hours, 11 minutes, and 14 seconds.*

PHOTOGRAPH FROM SUPPLEMENT TO THE NEW YORK *World*, FEBRUARY 2, 1890
THE NEW-YORK HISTORICAL SOCIETY

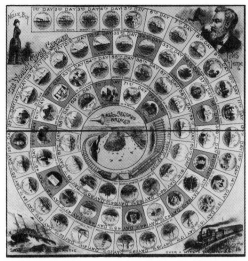

THE "NELLIE BLY"
GAMEBOARD

Played with a spinner and markers, the Nellie Bly game, manufactured in 1890 by McLoughlin Brothers of New York, was but one of many novelties inspired by the World's *globe-circling reporter. While songwriters set the story of Nellie's exploit to music, clothing stores were featuring a "Nellie Bly" dressing gown and hat. By her journey's end, one bemused commentator was wondering if the craze might not produce a "Nellie Bly" cigar as well.*
PARKER BROTHERS GAMES

Enlisting the Farmers: Mail Order and RFD

In the late nineteenth century, the great American railroad network combined with other forces to draw the remote farmer and his family into the new consumption communities. The American institutions which accomplished this were the mail-order houses. "Mail order," a new American expression, had come into general use by the beginning of the twentieth century. The consumption communities of Montgomery Ward or Sears buyers, which had not even existed at the end of the Civil War, a bare half-century later numbered millions. By the mid-twentieth century, Sears, Roebuck and Company would be the nation's largest retailer of general merchandise. This was a nationwide movement from the general store, with its gathering of a half-dozen local pundits around the cracker barrel, to the mail-order firm, with its dispersed customer-millions hungering through the half-thousand pages of vivid advertising copy, or waiting at their mailboxes.

Many farmers came to live more intimately with the Big Book of Ward's or Sears, Roebuck than with the Good Book. The farmer kept his Bible in the frigid parlor, but the latest mail-order catalog was commonly kept in the cozy kitchen, where the farm family ate and where they really lived. Some rural customers, without embarrassment, called the catalog "the Farmer's Bible." There was a familiar story of the little boy who was asked by his Sunday School teacher where the Ten Commandments came from and who unhesitatingly replied that they came from Sears, Roebuck.

The rise of mail order was another vivid allegory of how Americans were moving from cluster communities of transients and upstarts, of individuals calling one another by their first names, to a nation of everywhere communities of consumers and national-brand buyers who would never meet. Further stimulus to the mail-order business came with the adoption of Rural Free Delivery in the 1890's, opening paths from the remote farmers to an enormous warehouse of goods of all shapes and sizes.

AARON
MONTGOMERY
WARD
1843–1913

As a wholesale representative in the 1860's selling mostly to country merchants, Montgomery soon learned that farmers who traded at his clients' stores were victims of exorbitant prices and narrow selection. Out of this realization, Ward evolved his scheme for a wholesale mail-order house specifically geared to rural consumers. At first farmers regarded Ward's mail-order offerings with a good deal of suspicion. But a money-back guarantee combined with low prices and an ever-broadening selection of goods proved too good to pass up. By 1880 the semi-annual arrival of Ward's catalog was an eagerly awaited event in the nation's rural households.

FRANK O. SALISBURY, OIL ON CANVAS, AFTER 1900, 30″ × 26″
CHICAGO HISTORICAL SOCIETY, THE A. MONTGOMERY WARD FOUNDATION

54

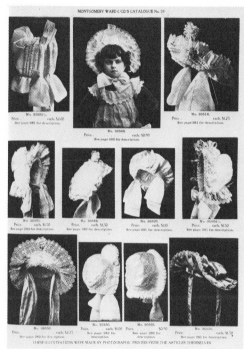

A WARNING TO
MAIL-ORDER
BUYERS

(left)
Unwilling to sit idly by while Ward's and Sears cut ever more deeply into their trade, many rural merchants fought back with flyers alerting customers to the hazards of mail-order buying. Nor were they above publicizing their cause with book-burnings in the town square. Their chief source of fuel: catalogs from Montgomery Ward and Sears, Roebuck.
MONTGOMERY WARD & CO.

WARD'S PRICE LIST,
CIRCA 1872

(center)
This one-page broadside is the earliest known Montgomery Ward catalog.
MONTGOMERY WARD & CO.

A PAGE FROM
MONTGOMERY
WARD'S SPRING
CATALOG, 1896

(right)
In 1896 Ward's began using photographed illustrations and live models in its catalogs. The hope, of course, was that a more literal presentation would stimulate sales. Sometimes, however, the customer was more taken with the model than with the merchandise. Such was the case when a farmer wrote to Ward's, proposing marriage to the "girl wearing hat number—on page 153."
MONTGOMERY WARD & CO.

**RICHARD WARREN
SEARS**
1863–1914

As a railroad station agent in rural Minnesota, Richard Sears was never averse to turning a quick profit on the side. In 1886, when a local jeweler left a watch shipment in the station with the freight costs unpaid, Sears paid the bill himself and began writing letters offering his newly acquired merchandise at bargain prices. By year's end he was in Minneapolis operating a mail-order watch company. Several years later, having gone into partnership with his watch repairer Alvah Roebuck, he was in Chicago looking for new ways to exploit the mail-order market. By the mid-nineties, the venture which began with some unclaimed watches had become a highly diversified merchandising house with yearly sales fast approaching the million-dollar mark.
PHOTOGRAPH, CIRCA 1886
SEARS, ROEBUCK AND CO.

56

ESTABLISHED MDCCCLXXXIV.

THE R. W. SEARS WATCH CO.

Manufacturers, Jobbers and Importers of

Watches, Diamonds and Jewelry,

51, 53 and 55 Dearborn Street,

CHICAGO, ILL.

To Our Patrons:

In presenting you with our Annual Illustrated Catalogue for 1888 and 1889, we embrace this opportunity of extending our sincere thanks for the very liberal support you have given us, and as an assurance of our appreciation, we place before you a complete line of American and Imported Watches which we are proud to say, for prices and variety, stand without an equal. Every illustration in this book is an exact representation of the article itself. Each cut being made from a photograph of the article; hence, you can order from this catalogue just as intelligently and with as much assurance of entire satisfaction as though you were at our store selecting the goods from stock.

We have studied carefully to avoid all exaggerations, honestly representing every thing, and any statement made concerning any article in this book is a correct one and fully guaranteed by us.

We want to hold the trade of our old customers and add as many new ones as possible. We do not claim as some do, to be the only honorable dealers in existence, or endowed with more power than other men, but we have a very extensive trade and buy in large quantities direct from the manufacturers, for cash, and we offer you every advantage that capital, skill and experience combined will command. A close comparison of our prices with those of other reliable houses will fully satisfy you that you can save money by placing your orders in our hands. We warrant every American watch sold by us, with fair usage, an accurate time keeper for six years—during which time, under our written guarantee we are compelled to keep it in perfect order free of charge.

(left)

CATALOG FROM
THE R. W. SEARS
WATCH COMPANY
1888-89

SEARS, ROEBUCK AND CO.

SEARS, ROEBUCK
CATALOG, 1894

(right)

By the mid-nineties the Ward and Sears catalogs had become thick, generously illustrated volumes numbering over 500 pages. As their size increased, so also did their uses. While mothers gave them to their children as a substitute for picture books, teachers in poorly equipped schools took to using the catalogs as the basis for lessons in reading, spelling, geography, and arithmetic.

SEARS, ROEBUCK AND CO.

ALVAH CURTIS
ROEBUCK
1864?-1948

Unlike Sears, Alvah C. Roebuck was not a driven man. "He's dead. Me, I never felt better," was his usual response when chided for selling out his share of their growing mail-order business for $20,000 in 1895; he later refused Sears' generous offer to take him back into the partnership. Although he had some success making motion pictures and speculating in Florida land, he was wiped out in the 1929 crash and spent the next ten years in the public relations department of Sears, Roebuck and Company.

PHOTOGRAPH, 1880's

SEARS, ROEBUCK AND CO.

JOHN WANAMAKER
1838-1922

No doubt Montgomery Ward and Richard Sears were elated when they learned in 1893 that Congress had finally approved funds for testing Postmaster General John Wanamaker's proposed system of Rural Free Delivery. If business was good now, what would it be like once their customers did not have to trek to town every time they wanted to place an order or pick up a new catalog? Aside from Ward, Sears, and the farmers they served, however, enthusiasm for rural mail routes was small. When Wanamaker left office in 1893 without implementing his trial run, Washington officialdom dropped the scheme. Only after 1896, when the agrarian-based Populist party threatened to cut into the strength of the two major parties, did politically minded postal officials take the first steps toward making RFD a reality.

UNIDENTIFIED ARTIST, OIL ON CANVAS, CIRCA 1894

DIVISION OF POSTAL HISTORY, THE NATIONAL MUSEUM OF HISTORY AND TECHNOLOGY, SMITHSONIAN INSTITUTION

RFD
AT WORK

Edwin Shriver delivering mail on the RFD route in Carroll County, Maryland, in 1899.
DIVISION OF POSTAL HISTORY, THE NATIONAL MUSEUM OF HISTORY AND TECHNOLOGY, SMITHSONIAN INSTITUTION

RURAL FREE
DELIVERY IN
LAFAYETTE,
INDIANA, CIRCA
1898

DIVISION OF POSTAL HISTORY, THE NATIONAL MUSEUM OF HISTORY AND TECHNOLOGY, SMITHSONIAN INSTITUTION

Popularizing the Tasteful Home

Mass merchandising was not the only factor whetting the consumer's appetite and giving impetus to the everywhere community. Also important was the rise of arbiters of national taste: these people instructed their followers through books, newspapers, and magazines, in the appropriateness of home appointments ranging from kitchen appliances to furniture and pictures on the wall. " 'Repent ye'," declared *Harper's Bazar* in the 1870's, mock-quoting one such arbiter, " 'For the Kingdom of the Tasteful is at hand!' "

CATHARINE
BEECHER
1800–1878

A childhood marked by stern Calvinism and emphasis on industry, and a youth shaken by the sudden death of her betrothed, led Catharine Beecher "to find happiness in living to do good." She devoted her considerable energies to securing equal educational opportunities for women and to promoting the study of domestic science.

She was instrumental in founding several women's colleges, and in recruiting capable teachers for them. In 1869 she collaborated with her sister Harriet Beecher Stowe to write The American Woman's Home, *an attempt to teach women how to organize domestic work and gain self-assurance in the profession of homemaking.*

THE STATE HISTORICAL SOCIETY OF WISCONSIN

61

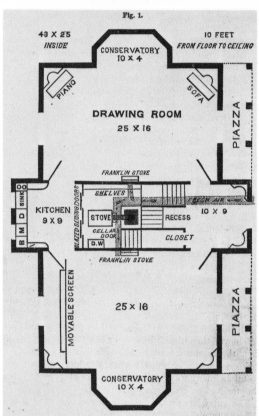

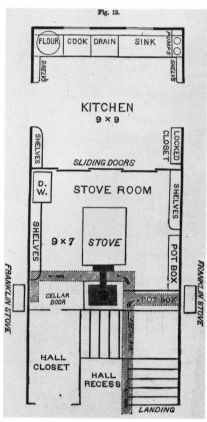

A DOMESTIC MASTER PLAN

Catharine Beecher and Harriet Beecher Stowe emphasized efficiency, comfort, and aesthetics in The American Woman's Home. *They wrote, for example, that the kitchen should be "so arranged that with one or two steps the cook can reach all he uses"—a drastic suggestion, because in most of that era's kitchens, "half the time and strength is employed in walking back and forth to collect and return the articles used."*

The kitchen, they advised, should be easily accessible to, yet separate from, both the stove room and the dining area; and it should be well ventilated. The sisters presented equally detailed plans for other rooms in the home.

FROM The American Woman's Home, or Principles of Domestic Science, 1869
LIBRARY OF CONGRESS

HARRIET BEECHER STOWE 1811–1896

Her first novel, Uncle Tom's Cabin, *gained Harriet Beecher Stowe fame that has overshadowed her copious, if less forceful, writings on a variety of other subjects. Beginning in 1852, she wrote, on the average, almost a book a year.*

In The American Woman's Home, *the sisters argued for "a moderate style of housekeeping, small, compact, and simple" and for the division among family members of as much of the household duties as was possible. No doubt Mrs. Stowe's experiences in raising six children contributed substantially to her knowledge of domestic economies.*

ALANSON FISHER, OIL ON CANVAS, 1853, 34″ × 26¾″

THE NATIONAL PORTRAIT GALLERY, SMITHSONIAN INSTITUTION

MAKERS OF STATISTICAL COMMUNITIES

Statistical communities, creatures of the new science of statistics, provided ways of clustering people into groups that made sense, without necessarily making undemocratic distinctions. The numbering of people (one person, one vote) itself seemed to symbolize the equality at which a democratic society aimed. From their very nature, numbers offered a *continuous* series, a refuge from those sharp leaps between "classes" found in other societies. And unlike the traditional categories of social class which had been topped by a divinely anointed monarch, statistical categories could be extended upward indefinitely. They were thus admirably adapted to a New World booster optimism: "The sky's the limit!" The direction of numbers, like the aims and hopes of American society, could go endlessly *up*.

A New Science of Numbers: The Census

A whole new science was coming into being for the quantitative analysis of society. The application to New World needs of theoretical tools from Western Europe was creating a new Numerical Science of Community. The words "statistics" and "statistical" entered the language in England about 1790, probably from the German. These new words, built on the word for "state," expressed expanding nationalism and also the universal quest for new "sciences," both of which bred a new faith in measurement.

Federal politics had committed us, from our national beginnings, to a special interest in numbers. At the Philadelphia Constitutional Convention in 1787 the large and the small states agreed on a two-branch federal legislature and established a House of Representatives where the people would be represented in proportion to population. "Representatives and direct Taxes shall be apportioned among the several States . . . according to their respective Numbers . . . the actual Enumeration shall be made three years after the first meeting of the Congress . . . and within every subsequent Term of ten Years . . ." (art. I, sec. 2, para. 3) The federal census was not the first such head count, but our periodic national census was probably the first in modern times to become institutionalized, and this American example influenced the world.

The census of 1790 counted only total population, divided into white (male and female) and "colored" (free and slave); white males were divided into those above and those below sixteen years of age. Even before the second census, a movement headed by the American Philosophical Society and led by Vice-President Thomas Jefferson urged a more detailed census to discover the facts about the life span of Americans so these could be used for devising social measures to promote longevity. But for the next half-century, census data continued to be gathered according to judicial districts by federal marshals who had no experience in such matters. The unit for gathering information was not the individual but the family.

The epoch-making seventh census of 1850, when the official statistics of the United States began to enter the modern era, was the product of a symbolic collaboration between two champions of statistics, one from the South and one from the North.

Eng⁴ by W.G. Jackman, N.Y.

JAMES D. B. DE BOW
1820–1867

James D. B. De Bow's brief tenure as census superintendent displayed none of the Southern partisanship that increasingly characterized his famous Review. *As chief of the short-lived Louisiana Bureau of Statistics, he gained national attention and was a logical choice to direct the 1850 census.*

The seventh census was the first to extend beyond general population enumeration and gather statistics for such areas as agriculture and manufacturing. De Bow hired specialists to interpret this information and then he summarized it in "A Statistical View of the United States." The quality of this work was unmatched for several decades, until De Bow's suggestion for a permanent census bureau was finally incorporated into law.

W. G. JACKMAN, ENGRAVING, IN *De Bow's Review*, JANUARY–JUNE, 1867
LIBRARY OF CONGRESS

LEMUEL SHATTUCK
1793–1859

Lemuel Shattuck's involvement with the 1850 census accounted for its attention to detail. Shattuck was responsible for founding the American Statistical Association in 1839, and for the passage three years later of a Massachusetts law requiring a uniform system of registering vital statistics. In 1845 he directed a census of Boston that enumerated individuals rather than families and noted characteristics such as national origin.

Shattuck's work was noticed by James D. B. De Bow, who summoned him to Washington to draft five of the six census schedules and write the instructions for the enumerators. The answers elicited by these enumerators made the seventh census a true national inventory rather than a haphazard collection of statistics.

UNIDENTIFIED ARTIST, ENGRAVING, DATE UNKNOWN
THE CONCORD ANTIQUARIAN SOCIETY, CONCORD, MASSACHUSETTS

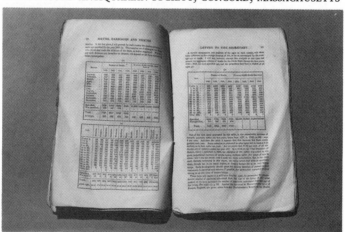

SHATTUCK'S TABLES OF VITAL STATISTICS

Lemuel Shattuck's tireless lobbying on behalf of legislation that established uniform registration of vital statistics made him a logical choice to evaluate the law's effectiveness. In a report addressed to the Massachusetts Secretary of State in 1846, he lauded the superior accuracy of recent records and demonstrated how they provided a wealth of new information about the state's residents.

FROM *Letter to the Secretary of State, on the Registration of Births, Marriages and Deaths, in Massachusetts,* BOSTON, 1846
LIBRARY OF CONGRESS

**HERMAN
HOLLERITH
1860-1929**

(left)
The mass of census information collected in the late nineteenth century made a mechanical means of processing statistical data highly desirable, and even necessary. By 1890, Dr. Herman Hollerith had invented a number of tabulating machines, one of which was selected for use in compiling the census.

Hollerith's machine recorded statistical items by a system of punched holes in paper cards, which were sorted for counting by the use of an electrical current. The machine's success—it cut by two-thirds the time needed to compile the 1890 census—led Hollerith to market it and join two other inventors in forming the company now known as IBM.

CABINET PHOTOGRAPH MADE BY GEORGE PRINCE, WASHINGTON, D.C., ABOUT 1890
THE MISSES HOLLERITH

**HOLLERITH'S
CENSUS
TABULATING
MACHINE**

(right)
SECTION OF MATHEMATICS, DEPARTMENT OF SCIENCE, THE NATIONAL MUSEUM OF
HISTORY AND TECHNOLOGY, SMITHSONIAN INSTITUTION

THE NEW CENSUS OF THE UNITED STATES—THE ELECTRICAL ENUMERATING MECHANISM.—[See page 132.]

HOLLERITH'S "ELECTRICAL ENUMERATING MACHINE"

The 1890 census data gathered by trained enumerators all over the nation were totaled by counting machines and separated into specific categories by tabulating machines. The accuracy of these machines greatly facilitated the work of interpreting just what all the numbers meant.
FROM *Scientific American*, AUGUST 30, 1890
SMITHSONIAN INSTITUTION LIBRARIES

68

Spreading the Risk: The Rise of Insurance

Of the new statistical communities, none was more widespread or more potent than the communities of the insured. By the mid-twentieth century, insurance touched the lives of all Americans, was a major item in the family budget, and shaped the American's vision of his future. In 1840 there was less than $5 million of life insurance (issued by a total of fifteen companies) in force in the whole United States. Within twenty

ELIZUR WRIGHT
1804–1885

Elizur Wright possessed a natural bent for reform. When even the most radical abolitionists found his views too extreme, he redirected his energies at the life insurance industry.

He found it "the most availably convenient and permanent nidus [nest] for rogues that civilization had ever presented," and successfully lobbied for laws eliminating the industry's worst abuses. Companies operating in Massachusetts were then required to maintain adequate reserves, were forbidden to appropriate reserves for their own uses, and were compelled to pay policyholders in cash for the full value of lapsed policies. As state insurance commissioner, he proved so diligent that the insurance companies successfully pressured the legislature to oust him by abolishing his office.

NEW ENGLAND MUTUAL LIFE INSURANCE COMPANY

years the face value of life policies exceeded $150 million; within another decade they reached $2 billion, and a century later totaled a staggering $1,284 billion. By 1970 there were 351 million life policies in force with an average coverage per family of $19,500. The assets of the fifty largest life insurance companies were valued at $164,555 million, and insurance companies had become a large factor in the investment and securities market and in the process of capital formation.

The prominence of insurance in American life, which historians seldom noted on paper, was starkly revealed on the American skyline. Insurance buildings rose in cathedral eminence. The history of the American skyscraper was embodied in monuments to the growing insurance industry, from the Equitable Life Building (1868–70) in New York through the Home Insurance Building (1883–85) in Chicago (the first skeleton-frame tall building, sometimes called the first true skyscraper) and the New York Life Insurance Building (1890) in Kansas City, and many others.

By its very nature, insurance—a new kind of consumption community—was a large-scale institution with a democratic reach. "While nothing is more uncertain than the duration of a single life," observed Elizur Wright, "nothing is more certain than the average duration of a thousand lives." Since insurance would not work for small numbers, it was necessarily a democratic commodity. So it was not surprising that the first flourishing of insurance into a gargantuan institution, rivaled in economic power only by government itself, came in the first large-scale democratic nation.

ELIZUR WRIGHT'S
ARITHMETER

The enormous number of calculations necessary in actuarial work led Elizur Wright to invent and patent the Arithmeter in 1869. The device mechanically adapted logarithmic principles, and was as accurate as an eighty-foot slide rule. With it, Wright was said to be able to do more than 250,000 calculations a year. Several insurance companies readily paid $600 for an Arithmeter, which guaranteed fast, accurate actuarial computations.
NEW ENGLAND MUTUAL LIFE INSURANCE COMPANY

HENRY B. HYDE
1834–1899

In 1859 the Equitable Life Assurance Society began its career as "protector of the widow and orphan" when Henry B. Hyde realized that none of the existing companies would insure an individual for more than $10,000.

Hyde hired Henry Ward Beecher to confute those who felt insurance implied a mistrust of God's plan and he advertised extensively in the religious press. His salesmen underwent elaborate training programs and attended annual sales conventions, among the first in the United States. Hyde's vigorous advertising and sales campaigns paid immediate dividends: after ten years of operation, Equitable stood third in policies in force; within thirty years, it was the world leader.

This statuette is a reduced replica of a large statue and is one of about eighty purchased from the sculptor for distribution to home offices of Hyde's insurance company.

JOHN QUINCY ADAMS WARD, BRONZE STATUETTE, CIRCA 1901, 20½″ HIGH
EQUITABLE LIFE ASSURANCE SOCIETY OF THE UNITED STATES

71

EQUITABLE'S NOTICE OF INTENT TO FORM A COMPANY, 1859

Building public trust was crucial to success in the insurance business. For this purpose, Henry B. Hyde enlisted some of New York's wealthiest bankers and merchants as incorporators for the Equitable Life Assurance Society. This notice of intent to form a company, issued by Hyde to satisfy a state law, listed these prominent men and was an effective initial advertisement.

EQUITABLE LIFE ASSURANCE SOCIETY OF THE UNITED STATES

EQUITABLE CIVIL WAR ADVERTISEMENT

Henry Hyde hoped to attract life insurance customers with this advertisement, featuring Army Chief of Staff Winfield Scott (left) and General George McClellan. No doubt President Lincoln's replacement of McClellan as commander in chief of the Army of the Potomac necessitated a hasty change in Equitable's advertising.

EQUITABLE LIFE ASSURANCE SOCIETY OF THE UNITED STATES

The Incorruptible Cashier: The Cash Register

Until well after the Civil War, it was the rare merchant who knew the precise amount of his income. Few had an accurate or detailed record of sales or of receipts. Though the proprietor of a general store, hoping for scrupulous accounts, might actually instruct his clerk to record everything in the daybook "even if the house was on fire," the clerk did not like to bother. Negligence, illiteracy, and laziness made the owner's record incomplete. There were overwhelming temptations to pilfer, especially where sales were numerous, and where the salesclerk or bartender made change from his own pocket or from an open cashbox. As a result, the merchant seldom knew precisely how much he had taken in during a day, how many sales there had been at different prices, or how much leakage of merchandise he was suffering due to negligence or dishonesty. In a word, he lacked the facts he needed to figure his income or his profit.

The device which did more than any other to change all this was the "cash register," an Americanism which entered the language about 1879, and which helped define the boundaries of new statistical communities. After the Sixteenth Amendment to the Constitution (1913), which empowered Congress to tax income from any source and without regard to population, a network of income-tax laws required each American to know his income, and so to become aware of his membership in another statistical community.

PATTERSON CASH REGISTER, MODEL 3, 1884

When John Patterson began manufacturing cash registers, they seemed to be an article nobody wanted. The value of a publicly registered sale punctuated with a ringing bell soon became apparent, however, and Patterson's fortunes began to build. The "thief catcher" eliminated the open cash drawer and in the process frustrated many a clerk who had supplemented a meager income by dipping into the till.
NATIONAL CASH REGISTER CORPORATION, PATENT AND HISTORICAL SERVICES

JOHN HENRY
PATTERSON
1844–1922

Forced in 1884 to make the best of what seemed a bad $6,500 investment in a local cash register company, Dayton businessman John H. Patterson launched the "American Selling Force" to market his product.

Salesmen underwent thorough evangelical training sessions and were provided with standardized sales talks, sales quotas for guaranteed territories, and the incentive of straight commissions. Factory workers benefited from a comprehensive industrial welfare system and a profit-sharing plan. Patterson, however, demanded strict discipline: company executives, for example, were expected to join him in his 5 A.M. calisthenics. The Patterson mixture of motivation and discipline won for him the nickname of "Cash" and, by 1910, gained 90 percent of the market for his National Cash Register Company.

J. PHILLIP SCHMAND, OIL ON CANVAS, 1920, 30″ × 25″

NATIONAL PORTRAIT GALLERY, SMITHSONIAN INSTITUTION, GIFT OF THE
PATTERSON MEMORIAL THROUGH MRS. MARVIN BRECKINRIDGE PATTERSON

Statistical Morality

In Western Europe, the last years of the nineteenth century and the early years of the twentieth century brought new attitudes toward sex among a vanguard few. By 1900 Sigmund Freud had published his basic works on psychoanalysis. In 1909, when G. Stanley Hall brought Freud, who was then still slightly disreputable in European scientific circles, to

G. STANLEY HALL
1844–1924

G. Stanley Hall shifted the focus of American education from the needs of the school to those of the child. Under the influence of William James and several German psychologists, Hall launched the "Child Study Movement." His innovative book, The Contents of Children's Minds *(1883), used questionnaires to discover both what children actually knew and what they did not* know. *Hall saw psychic life as an evolutionary process repeating the history of mankind's rise: children were not corrupt, but primitive. It was essential to understand what was "natural" for them. "Norms" replaced moral rules for Hall and his disciples, who set out to discover and define normal behavior.*
FREDERICK VINTON, OIL ON CANVAS, DATE UNKNOWN, 54″ × 42″
CLARK UNIVERSITY ARCHIVES, WORCESTER, MASSACHUSETTS

a conference at Clark University in Worcester, Massachusetts, Hall caused a stir, but it helped make Freud more respectable in America than he was in his home country. The increasingly free—and increasingly statistical—American attitude toward sex was expressed in Dr. Alfred C. Kinsey's book *Sexual Behavior in the Human Male,* which was published in 1948 and quickly made the best-seller list. The book's avowed purpose was "an accumulation of scientific fact completely divorced from questions of moral value and social custom." As the truths about American sexual behavior (diffused by the works of Kinsey and others) took the form of quantitative, scientifically authenticated norms, there was a tendency among Americans for morality to be replaced by "normality."

PSYCHOANALYTICAL PARTICIPANTS IN CLARK UNIVERSITY PSYCHOLOGY CONFERENCE, 1909

As the first president of Clark University, Hall struggled to make it the national center for Psychology and Child Study, despite opposition from the founder and financial mainstay, Jonas Gilman Clark. Hall brought the notorious Sigmund Freud to the 1909 Psychology Conference held to commemorate Clark's twentieth anniversary; there Freud gave his first American lectures. Through Hall's later writings as much as his own, Freud's ideas won increasing acceptance in America.
CLARK UNIVERSITY ARCHIVES, WORCESTER, MASSACHUSETTS

Hall pioneered in another respect as well: the introduction of statistics to the study of children. The child-study movement sought to discover what children were actually like, what they felt and thought, how they developed. Statistical norms for growth and behavior made the word "naughty" seem quaint. As Americans became child-centered, they were less inclined to moralize about what might, after all, only be "normal" for the child to do.

Morality took another sharp turn with the rise of "scientific management" and the adaptation, by Frederick Taylor and Frank and Lillian Gilbreth, of cameras and other devices to the study of work. Time-and-motion study meant evaluating performance on the basis of efficiency as well as quality; waste was the cardinal sin. With the acceptance of the concept of the "one best way" to do a task, work moved toward an objective standard of value never before possible.

BOAS' STATISTICAL QUESTIONNAIRE

(left)
In the 1890's Franz Boas, a young German "anthropometrist" brought to Clark University by Hall, measured thousands of Worcester schoolchildren for rate of growth, memory, vision, and hearing. The wide range of variations among "healthy" children disappointed Hall's hope of discovering statistical "norms" by which "diseased" or "subnormal" children could be isolated; such studies, however, ultimately did lead to better-designed schoolroom furniture and other advances.
CLARK UNIVERSITY ARCHIVES, WORCESTER, MASSACHUSETTS

FUND-RAISING LETTER FOR SECOND CHILD CONFERENCE FOR RESEARCH AND WELFARE, 1910

(right)
Once Americans became aware of the existence of "children" and "adolescents" and conscious of their distinct needs, Child Welfare started to become a political and social issue. Hall, a tireless letter-writer and organizer, formed a natural bridge between the academics—many of them his disciples—studying children, and the reformers—such as Jacob Riis and "Children's Judge" Ben Lindsey—trying to help them.
CLARK UNIVERSITY ARCHIVES, WORCESTER, MASSACHUSETTS

77

ALFRED CHARLES
KINSEY
1894–1956

After twenty years of studying individual variations among insect populations, biologist Alfred C. Kinsey turned in 1938 to a problem little investigated by science—individual variations in sexual behavior among the human population. "The technique we are using in this study," he wrote in 1944, "is definitely the same as the technique in the gall wasp study"—that is, to collect and analyze as many specimens as possible. The microscope by which Kinsey and his staff gently scrutinized human subjects was the interview-questionnaire: "We always assume that everyone has engaged in every type of activity." Kinsey's tirelessness in search of truth, his refusal to presuppose or moralize about his findings, and his integrity all made him an ideal person to break the news that a sexual revolution was under way.

BORIS ARTZYBASHEFF, REPRODUCED AS THE COVER OF *Time,* AUGUST 24, 1953, GOUACHE ON BOARD, 11¾″ × 9″(SIGHT)
INSTITUTE FOR SEX RESEARCH, INC., INDIANA UNIVERSITY

"Mr. Tilby is in the Kinsey Report."

TWO 1948 REACTIONS TO "THE KINSEY REPORT"

After a quarter-century, it is difficult to recall America before Kinsey. Rejected by one publisher as too dry to reach more than a limited audience, Sexual Behavior in the Human Male *(1948) became a colossal best seller. But its once-shocking revelations have long since ceased to be controversial.*

The concealed copy in Herb Williams' cartoon was both comic and common; the plain brown wrapper that once clothed pornography and marriage manuals now garbed Kinsey. The woman's alarmed expression probably arises from suspicion that her husband, like millions of American men, was "guilty" of behavior considered "abnormal," "deviant," wrong, or at least rare, before Kinsey. Mr. Tilby, in Gardner Rea's drawing, may have been one of the sexual heroes discovered by Kinsey who entered American folklore.

"MR. TILBY" BY GARDNER REA, FROM *True*, 1948. COPYRIGHT BY FAWCETT PUBLICATIONS, INC.

"HOME GARDENER" BY HERB WILLIAMS, JANUARY 4, 1948. COPYRIGHT BY THE NEW YORK TIMES COMPANY. REPRINTED BY PERMISSION.

LILLIAN MOLLER
GILBRETH
1878–1972

Lillian Moller's marriage to Frank B. Gilbreth in 1904 inaugurated a remarkable collaboration. A psychologist, Lillian Gilbreth added a human dimension to their scientific management consultancy business. Together they pioneered in time and motion study, using moving pictures and developing measurement devices, such as the "chronocyclograph." They coined the term "therblig" (Gilbreth spelled backwards—almost) and used this unit of work and motion to determine the "one best way" of doing each task. Going beyond improving industrial productivity and the efficiency of work, the Gilbreths studied the handicapped to find ways to make them self-sufficient. After her husband's death in 1924, Lillian Gilbreth continued this work as well as publishing extensively on home management and child-raising.
FRANK STANLEY HERRING, OIL ON CANVAS, 1930, 40″ × 30″
ERNESTINE GILBRETH CAREY

THE GILBRETH
FAMILY LESS TWO

The Gilbreths' parental achievements rivaled their business and scientific ones, as two best-selling books and films made from them have shown (Cheaper by the Dozen *and* Belles on Their Toes). *Millions of Americans are familiar with Frank Gilbreth's efforts to manage scientifically an eleven-child household (one child died young), and with his wife's efforts after his death at age fifty-six.*
PHOTOGRAPH TAKEN IN MONTCLAIR, NEW JERSEY, 1921
FRANK GILBRETH

STRETCHING THE CITY

Men and women in everywhere communities were not quite sure where they were living. The Old World peasant's traditional affection was for the *land* of his forefathers, the village where parents and grandparents were buried in the churchyard. But merely by coming to America, an immigrant had shown his willingness to move. Inevitably, when he first arrived he found himself in a city, and many of the most numerous immigrant groups remained city dwellers.

The American city, the marketing center of consumption communities, the information center of statistical communities, was the special

81

scene of a new rooting and uprooting. Most men before had been attached to the soil, inspirited by the sunshine and sky and trees and birds of some particular corner of the earth. That sense of place Americans now sought to rediscover in their corner of cemented sidewalks, on macadamed rectilinear streets, among geometric skyscrapers.

Streetcar Suburbs

Before the coming of the streetcar, a city's natural boundaries had extended only to the distance that a man could walk from the center in about an hour. For among city dwellers, horses and carriages were mostly for the rich. The steam railroad which went to a central station had enlarged the trading area of the city but did not provide transportation for short distances, and so did not change the pattern of daily life. The "streetcar" (an Americanism which came into use about the time of the Civil War) made it possible for someone who could not afford a private carriage to work in the city and live outside.

The new "streetcar suburbs" (as historian Sam B. Warner, Jr., calls them) did not take the city out of focus, but they were the beginning of the end of the walking city. Boston, for example, which as late as 1850 was still a pedestrian city with a mere three-mile radius, had by 1900 become a suburbanized metropolis with a ten-mile radius. The instrument of this transformation was the streetcar.

STEPHENSON CAR
COMPANY, 1889

By 1889, when the above photograph was taken, John Stephenson's factory in New York was clearly outmoded. The ceilings were too low for the assembly of the new electric cars, and the floor beams sagged dangerously under the added weight of electric motors. A new factory in Patterson, New Jersey, was built too late to save the company from bankruptcy.
MUSEUM OF THE CITY OF NEW YORK

82

JOHN STEPHENSON
1809–1893

Half a century after John Stephenson had introduced the horse-drawn omnibus to New York in 1831, millions of people from Bombay to Sioux City rode in streetcars built by his company. Stephenson's preeminence was based on superior craftsmanship and a perceptive reading of the revolution in urban transit.

The Stephenson Company produced omnibuses until the 1850's, when it was converted for production of the increasingly popular streetcar. The introduction of electric and cable power in the late 1880's, however, exposed the outmoded features of Stephenson's factory, which was unequipped to meet the demand for bigger, heavier cars. Competitors quickly captured the market and shortly after Stephenson's death, his company went bankrupt.

PHOTOGRAPH BY NAEGELI, DATE UNKNOWN
MUSEUM OF THE CITY OF NEW YORK

ADVERTISING CARD FOR THE STEPHENSON COMPANY, 1873

In 1832 John Stephenson built the "John Mason" for the New York & Harlem Railroad. Unlike his first omnibus of the previous year, the "John Mason" was mounted on flange wheels that ran on tracks rather than the rough, unpaved city streets. Comparison with the Broadway 323 shows the changes Stephenson made in the design of his horse-drawn streetcars over a fifty-year period.
DIVISION OF TRANSPORTATION, THE NATIONAL MUSEUM OF HISTORY AND TECHNOLOGY, SMITHSONIAN INSTITUTION

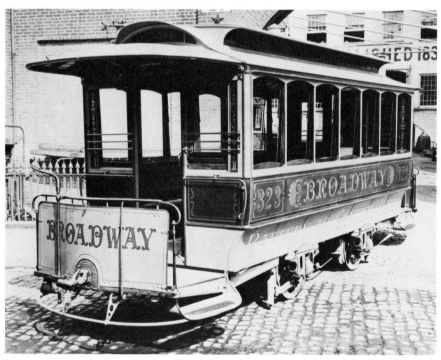

THE BROADWAY 323 STREETCAR

The Broadway 323, delivered in 1886, was the largest, most luxurious style of horsecar built by the Stephenson Company. It featured upholstered seats, kerosene lighting, and a fare register to count passengers. The streetcar line it serviced carried nearly thirty million passengers annually over an eight-mile route.
JOHN STEPHENSON COMPANY ALBUM, 1888
DIVISION OF TRANSPORTATION, THE NATIONAL MUSEUM OF HISTORY AND TECHNOLOGY, SMITHSONIAN INSTITUTION

84

GEORGE
WESTINGHOUSE
1846-1914

George Westinghouse combined a versatile inventive genius with a shrewd sense of how to exploit his inventions financially. The introduction of his airbrake in 1869 considerably reduced the hazards of rail travel because it enabled the engineer safely to brake all the train's cars simultaneously.

In 1885 Westinghouse purchased the patent rights to the development of a transformer that enabled safe, widespread use of alternating current to transmit electric power. Concurrently he developed a system of successively larger pipes for the safe transmission of natural gas from well to consumer. These and other inventions gave birth to a huge industrial complex: at various times Westinghouse controlled forty companies worth more than $200 million and employing fifty thousand people.

DANIEL CHESTER FRENCH, BRONZE, 1925, 32″ HIGH
DIVISION OF ELECTRICITY AND NUCLEAR ENERGY, THE NATIONAL MUSEUM OF HISTORY AND TECHNOLOGY, SMITHSONIAN INSTITUTION

85

MODEL OF
STANLEY
TRANSFORMER, 1885

The Stanley transformer, developed under George Westinghouse in 1885, allowed the general use of electricity. The direct current then in use required large amounts of wire and could be sent only in low voltages over short distances. Transformers permitted the use of alternating current, which could be sent in high voltages for great distances over small wires and then "stepped down" or transformed to the low voltage necessary for safe local use.

BERKSHIRE MUSEUM, PITTSFIELD, MASSACHUSETTS

HENRY M. WHITNEY
1839–1923

Henry M. Whitney was the first traction magnate fully to exploit electricity as a motive force when, in 1886, he linked Brookline to Boston with a streetcar line. Whitney next consolidated the numerous Boston street railway companies and extended suburban railway lines by maintaining five-cent fares and free transfers.

Unfortunately, he impoverished the inner-city streetcar lines in order to provide rapid, extensive suburban service, which he believed would encourage suburban home ownership. In 1897 a group of businessmen, pledged to provide convenient service to both city and suburb, forced Whitney to lease his entire system to them.

ALEXANDER HAY RITCHIE, ENGRAVING, DATE UNKNOWN
NATIONAL PORTRAIT GALLERY, SMITHSONIAN INSTITUTION

**HENRY E.
HUNTINGTON
1850–1927**

The urban sprawl which characterizes modern Los Angeles received its initial impulse from the designs of Henry E. Huntington. In 1900, after inheriting a vast fortune from his uncle, Huntington began to extend streetcar lines in all directions from Los Angeles. Simultaneously he purchased thousands of acres of real estate along the lines and began developing residential and resort communities. In this way Huntington constantly recouped the cost of his car lines through the sale of his real estate.

Eventually his streetcar lines, valued at $100 million in 1910, extended thirty-five miles from the city, serving at least forty incorporated communities and adding twelve new suburbs to metropolitan Los Angeles. In this photograph, taken about 1922, Huntington is standing at the door of his library in San Marino, California.

HUNTINGTON LIBRARY, SAN MARINO, CALIFORNIA

HUNTINGTON
INSPECTING HIS
EMPIRE

"Mr. Turner," Henry E. Huntington and George Clinton Ward, a principal railway associate, on the tracks of the San Joaquin & Eastern Railroad, one of Huntington's many suburban lines.
PHOTOGRAPH, 1914
HUNTINGTON LIBRARY, SAN MARINO, CALIFORNIA

ORIS P. VAN
SWERINGEN
1879–1936
AND
MANTIS J. VAN
SWERINGEN
1881–1935

*"I can't recall the time when I lost anything by keeping my mouth shut,"
remarked Oris Van Sweringen when explaining why he and his brother Mantis
were so tight-lipped about their business dealings. Gaining an initial financial
foothold with their development of Shaker Heights—a four-thousand-acre
Cleveland suburb featuring romantic landscaping and numerous restrictive
covenants—they turned next to railroad investment.*

*After acquiring the Nickel Plate Line in 1916 to provide rapid-transit service
to Shaker Heights, they built an investment pyramid of holding companies that
controlled twenty-eight thousand miles of track and had assets of $4 billion.
Unfortunately, their empire was built of paper and collapsed when they were
unable to meet payments on millions of dollars of loans during the depths of the
Depression.*

ALFRED JONNIAUX, OIL ON CANVAS, 1929, 43″ × 34″
THE SHAKER HISTORICAL SOCIETY, SHAKER HEIGHTS, OHIO

FREDERICK LAW
OLMSTED
1822–1903

Though many American cities bear his imprint, Frederick Law Olmsted is best known for designing Central Park in New York City. His initial venture in landscape architecture included such innovations as the separation of vehicular from pedestrian traffic and led to a forty-year career planning parks, suburbs, campuses, and private estates all over the United States. While respecting nature, he rearranged natural elements in all of his designs, to produce a usable, yet romantic, landscape.

Olmsted's talents as both artist and engineer were aptly described by architect Daniel Burnham, who wrote: "He paints with lakes and wooded slopes; with lawns and banks and forest-covered hills; with mountainsides and ocean views."

JOHN SINGER SARGENT, OIL ON CANVAS, 1895, 96″ × 72″

BILTMORE HOUSE AND GARDENS, ASHEVILLE, NORTH CAROLINA

OLMSTED'S FIELD   DR. AND MRS. STEPHEN P. GILL
CAMERA

OLMSTED'S   DR. AND MRS. STEPHEN P. GILL
DRAFTING
INSTRUMENTS

VIEW OF CENTRAL   *Only seven years after the Greensward Plan for Central Park was selected, most*
PARK, SUMMER 1865   *of the landscaping had been completed. This view of the park in 1865 shows a*
formal area of promenade, lake, and fountain surrounded by less formal pathways
and meadows. Not until later did the city reach north of Fifty-ninth Street to
envelop the park with skyscrapers.
J. BEIN AFTER JOHN BACHMANN, COLORED LITHOGRAPH, 1865
MUSEUM OF THE CITY OF NEW YORK, J. CLARENCE DAVIES COLLECTION

91

PRESENT OUTLINES.

EFFECT PROPOSED.

PAGE OF
GREENSWARD PLAN,
FOR CENTRAL
PARK, 1858

Frederick Law Olmsted and Calvert Vaux enhanced their winning entry in the 1858 design competition for Central Park with a series of watercolor views of how certain areas of the park would look. They juxtaposed these with photographs of the same views, to underline the changes they planned. As one of these before-and-after comparisons reveals, Olmsted and Vaux planned to transform a rocky, gully-creased landscape into one of tree-covered slopes and lakes.
MUSEUM OF THE CITY OF NEW YORK

JESSE C. NICHOLS
1880–1950

Realizing that "the most attractive headline . . . for an advertisment [for real estate] is 'on a boulevard' or 'near a boulevard,'" Jesse C. Nichols shrewdly catered to the public interest in Kansas City's program of civic beautification when he developed his Country Club District. Several wide boulevards built by the city linked the six-thousand-acre suburb to the city and its burgeoning system of public parks. Restrictive covenants guaranteed wealthy home owners a tasteful architectural conformity.

The truly distinctive feature of Nichols' development, however, was the construction of the nation's first suburban shopping center. The Country Club Plaza, opened in 1922, was soon copied and touted as another in the growing list of conveniences of suburban living.

PHOTOGRAPH, NOVEMBER 17, 1922

JACKSON COUNTY HISTORICAL SOCIETY ARCHIVES, INDEPENDENCE, MISSOURI, STRAUSS-PEYTON COLLECTION

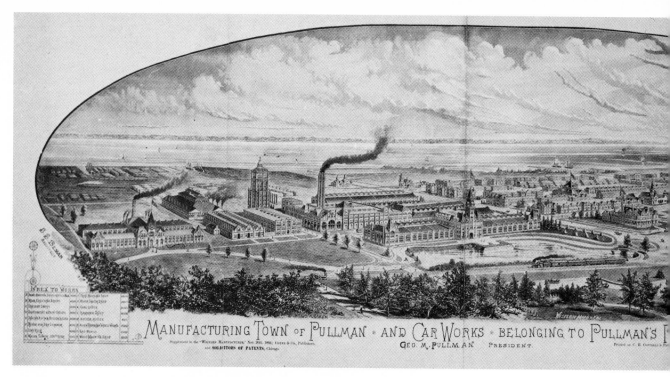

MANUFACTURING TOWN OF PULLMAN · AND CAR WORKS · BELONGING TO PULLMAN'S
GEO. M. PULLMAN   PRESIDENT.

TOWN OF PULLMAN   *A view of Pullman from a supplement to* Western Manufacturer *(November 30, 1881), published by Coyne & Company, Chicago.*
THE CHICAGO HISTORICAL SOCIETY

Antidotes for the City

The vagueness of the city compounded ancient problems and led Americans at first to search for remedies, then to reach for antidotes. Some tried importing Old World schemes of paternalist utopia. Others hoped that old ills could be cured by "renewal," by trying to erase what was there and beginning all over again. By the mid-twentieth century the future seemed to lie with refugees from the city who were finding new ways to make suburbs into communities.

In the nineteenth century some Americans had devised American versions of the English or continental model industrial town. These were distinguished by the simplicity and coherence of their plans, by the paternalism of their government, and by their initial, short-run success and long-run failure. Early in the century, New Englanders like Francis Cabot Lowell had built model towns to house their workers, elevate their minds, and protect their morals. Later in the century the most impressive and best advertised of such efforts was Pullman, Illinois, a model community outside Chicago, named after its founder, shaper, and ruler, George M. Pullman.

Among those who were unhappy with how American cities had grown were many who opposed the paternalism of the "company town." They believed that there were values in city life which could not be reproduced in artificial utopian villages. Their hope was to rid the cities of poverty, crime, prostitution, and disease, and they made slums their special target.

94

GEORGE M. PULLMAN 1831–1897

By constructing a model town for his workers, George Pullman hoped to avoid the labor troubles endemic to the late nineteenth century. Despite its physical amenities, the Pullman experiment was doomed by the domineering, uncompromising character of its maker. He viewed the community more as a business venture than a philanthropic gesture. Rents, calculated to return a generous 6 percent, were 25 percent higher than those in surrounding communities. The rigid rules governing town life led one observer to describe the town as "benevolent well-wishing feudalism."

In 1894 the strike Pullman feared materialized when he refused to match a pay cut with a rent cut. The use of federal troops to repress the strike marked the end of his experiment.

EASTMAN JOHNSON, OIL ON CANVAS, CIRCA 1878, 59″ × 38¾″

THE CHICAGO HISTORICAL SOCIETY, MRS. FRANK O. LOWDEN

(FLORENCE SANGER PULLMAN)

SOLON S. BEMAN
1853–1914

George Pullman chose Solon S. Beman, an untried New York architect, to design his model community and gave him virtually unlimited resources and control. Beman, who was responsible not only for architectural design but also for business management and engineering, spent $12 million to build a much-lauded town-and-factory complex.

He mixed housing by including detached houses, row houses, and apartments, and designed a park and sanitation system that significantly lowered the incidence of disease. Unfortunately, Beman's innovative plan could not rescue the Pullman experiment from the socioeconomic factors that led to its failure. Beman subsequently enjoyed a successful career in Chicago and helped design the World's Columbian Exposition of 1893.

OLIVER DENNETT GROVER, OIL ON CANVAS, 1911, 40¼″ × 37¼″

THE CHICAGO HISTORICAL SOCIETY, THE CHICAGO CHAPTER, THE AMERICAN INSTITUTE OF ARCHITECTS

96

VIEW WEST ON 112TH STREET, PULLMAN

This view of Pullman shows the Greenstone Church (left), for many years the only one Pullman allowed to be built in the town, and the Arcade (upper right). The sharp contrast between the row houses (left center) and the more sumptuous dwelling opposite the church is an eloquent reminder of the social and economic distinctions that separated laborer from manager in Pullman.
THE CHICAGO HISTORICAL SOCIETY

ARCADE PARK, PULLMAN

Though Arcade Park was too formal to permit anything but leisurely strolling, the surrounding buildings made it a center of town activity. The Hotel Florence (upper left) housed the many visitors who came to view the model community. The Arcade (on left, not shown) contained offices, shops, the bank, the theater, and the library. The row houses on the remaining two sides of the park housed employees of the car works.
THE CHICAGO HISTORICAL SOCIETY

JACOB A. RIIS
1849–1914

When Jacob Riis started as a reporter in 1877, the slum was a grim but accepted reality of urban life. He spent the next three decades photographically documenting tenement life and seeking to eliminate its worst abuses. Self-interest, if not human decency, argued Riis, necessitated such action: "Either we wipe out the slum, or it wipes us out."

His campaign, which enlisted such supporters as Theodore Roosevelt, secured adequate lighting for tenement hallways, forced the destruction of rear tenements, and secured playgrounds and parks for tenement residents. His reforms, unlike many of his era, had an immediate and tangible impact on a social problem plaguing American cities.

PHOTOGRAPH, CIRCA 1910

MUSEUM OF THE CITY OF NEW YORK

"FLASHES FROM THE SLUMS," 1888 *Much of the impact of Jacob Riis's crusade against the slum can be traced to his photographs of slum life. Reproduced as line engravings in his newspaper articles, Riis's pictures proved more eloquent than words in conveying the wretched despair of the slum dweller, and were instrumental in gaining him the support of many influential citizens. Those illustrated here appeared in the February 12, 1888, edition of the New York Sun under the title "Flashes from the Slums."*

Street Arabs in night quarters on Mulberry Street

Rushing the Growler

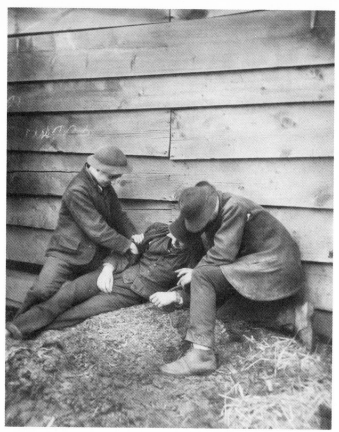

Hell's Kitchen boys "showing their trick" (how they roll drunks)

Baxter Street Court, 22 Baxter Street

Baxter Street Alley

The Short Tail Gang under the pier at the foot of Jackson Street

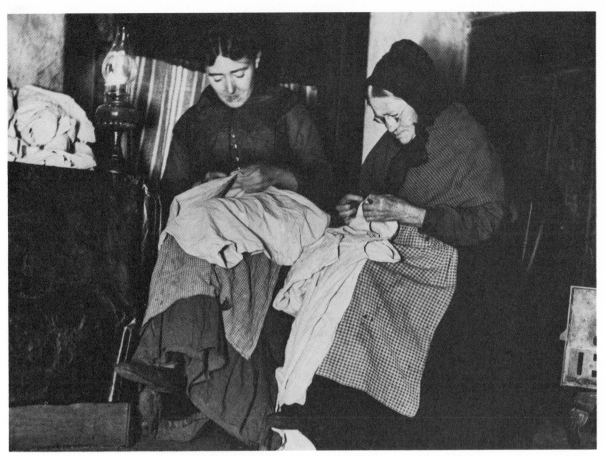

Two sewing women in their attic room

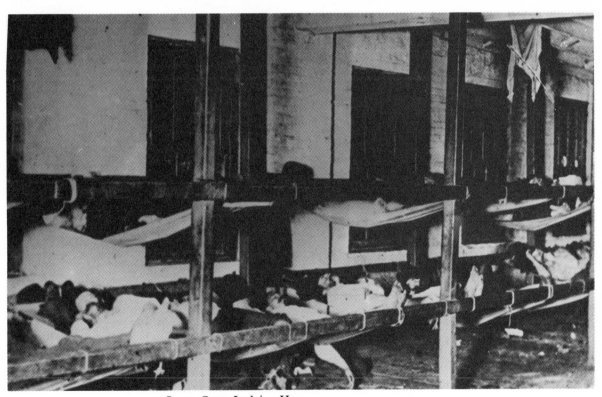

Seven Cents Lodging House

101

Cities within Cities

Negro Americans, even if they had the money, were not free to join the idyllic suburb of their choice, nor to enter the everywhere community of suburbanites. From their early arrival on the scene of American History, Negro Americans had an experience not shared by other Americans. Even after emancipation, after a bloody civil war which purported to bring the Negro into the community of free Americans, the Negro remained an indelible immigrant, prevented in numerous ways from taking his rightful place in the large community.

In the Age of Everywhere Communities, when cities had become centers of movement and mobility, when Americans were freely joining and leaving consumption communities, when they were being grouped by their interpreters and by themselves in fast-changing statistical communities, when neighborhoods had been dissolved in the vagueness of the city, when even the boundaries between city and countryside had become uncertain, the Negro still found himself marked off and confined.

As other Americans moved cityward, so did the Negro. The Negro's cityward migration was also a migration out of the South. The proportion of the nation's Negro population found in the South declined from 90 percent in 1870 to 60 percent in 1960. Negroes living in the rural South generally did not move to a Southern city on their way northward and westward. The dispersion out into the nation showed a striking uniformity.

The Negro's immigration to the city was one more American saga—as full of adventure, of hope and disappointment as any of the other migrations that had built the nation. But at that stage, too, certain features sharply distinguished the Negro's experience. Other immigrant groups—the Irish, the Italians, the Jews—had generally begun their American experience in their own gathered community in a city. In the South, however, the Negro had been primarily a rural person; he had generally lived in small groups dispersed among the white population, to serve the convenience of his white master or employer.

When the Negro migrant arrived at his Promised Land outside the South, segregation ordinances, social pressures, and fear, and then inevitable choice, kept him confined in his own city within the city. Negro communities developed a life of their own, with their own character, their own glamour, and their own frustrations. By 1920 the Negro population of New York City, overwhelmingly concentrated in Harlem, numbered more than 150,000, making it the largest Negro community in the nation. Within the next decade, the remarkable group of literary, musical, and artistic talents which flourished there had brought to that repossessed slum a world-wide reputation.

ALAIN LOCKE
1886–1954

A professor at Howard University in Washington, D.C., Alain Locke lived far from Harlem. In spirit, however, he was at its very center as it became the Mecca of the Black cultural flowering in the 1920's. His compilation of Black writings, The New Negro *(1925), became a basic reference point for interpreting the period's outburst of creativity, and Harlem artists and writers discovered in him an invaluable friend, critic, and patron. For many of them, his anthologies and essays, in which time and again he urged the Black artist to seek both the substance and form of expression within his own racial heritage, were vital forces in the shaping of their work.*

WINOLD REISS, PASTEL ON ARTIST BOARD, CIRCA 1925, 29⅞″ × 21⅝″
NATIONAL PORTRAIT GALLERY, SMITHSONIAN INSTITUTION

JAMES WELDON
JOHNSON
1871–1938

Despite heavy responsibilities throughout the 1920's as secretary of the NAACP, James Weldon Johnson found time for literary pursuits. Believing with Locke that the Black artist must look to his racial heritage for inspiration, Johnson began exploring America's Black traditions in his own work in 1918, after listening to a sermon delivered by a Black evangelist. Deeply moved, he started a series of poems known as God's Trombones, *in which he captured the rhythmic cadences of Black preaching. Through his anthologies and critical essays, Johnson also did much to win recognition for many of the era's younger writers, among them Claude McKay and Langston Hughes.*

WINOLD REISS, PASTEL ON ARTIST BOARD, CIRCA 1925, 30$^{1}/_{16}''$ × 21$^{9}/_{16}''$
NATIONAL PORTRAIT GALLERY, SMITHSONIAN INSTITUTION

104

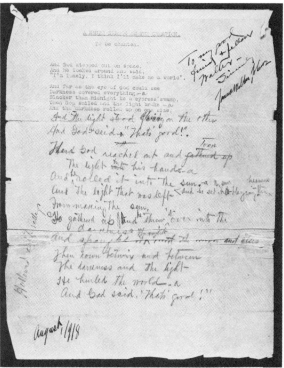

ILLUSTRATION
FROM *THE NEW
NEGRO* (1925) BY
AARON DOUGLAS

(left)
The African motif adopted by Aaron Douglas in his illustrations for The New
Negro *reflected Locke's hope that Black sculptors and painters would draw their
inspiration from African art. "The legacy is there," Locke observed, "with
prospects for a rich yield."*
LIBRARY OF CONGRESS

A PAGE FROM AN
EARLY DRAFT OF
JAMES WELDON
JOHNSON'S
"CREATION," 1918

(right)
*"The Creation" was the first in the series of poems which in 1927 were published
under the title* God's Trombones. *Describing the Kansas City preacher who
inspired it, Johnson later wrote: "He strode the pulpit up and down, and brought
into play the full gamut of a voice that excited my envy. He intoned, he moaned,
he pleaded—he blared, he crashed, he thundered . . . I was fascinated . . . something
primordial in me stirred." Before the sermon was over, Johnson was jotting down
the ideas for his poem.*
THE JAMES WELDON JOHNSON MEMORIAL COLLECTION OF NEGRO ARTS AND
LETTERS, COLLECTION OF AMERICAN LITERATURE, THE BEINECKE RARE BOOKS AND
MANUSCRIPT LIBRARY, YALE UNIVERSITY

LANGSTON HUGHES
1902-1967

Langston Hughes gained literary recognition in 1926 with the publication of his volume of poems entitled The Weary Blues. *One of the most prolific and versatile of the Harlem writers, Hughes was often criticized by blacks and whites alike for concentrating on the more unpleasant aspects of Black life in his poems, novels, and short stories. Still, throughout his works there ran an optimism, humor, and pride in race, which transcended the bitter realities he portrayed. "I am the darker brother," he once wrote. "They send me to eat in the kitchen/ When company comes,/ But I laugh,/ And eat well,/ And grow strong./ Tomorrow,/ I'll be at the table . . ."*

WINOLD REISS, PASTEL ON ARTIST BOARD, CIRCA 1925, 30¹/₁₆″ × 21⅝″
NATIONAL PORTRAIT GALLERY, SMITHSONIAN INSTITUTION

106

CLAUDE MCKAY
1889–1948

A native of Jamaica, Claude McKay sounded one of Harlem's earliest notes of racial militancy in 1919 with the publication of his poem "If I Must Die." Like Hughes, McKay did not skirt the less palatable aspects of the Black experience in his work. His novel, Home to Harlem *(1928), which depicted the New York community's low life, drew heavy fire from figures such as W. E. B. Du Bois, who felt that Black writers should stress only the more positive elements of the Black community. Langston Hughes, on the other hand, regarded it as "the first real flower of the Harlem Renaissance."*
LIBRARY OF CONGRESS

S. O. S.
May 4, 1926.
LINCOLN UNIVERSITY, PA.

Dear Friend,

Comme toujours, my pockets are terribly empty. Could you send me a ten until the Herald Tribune pays for my Blues they took? It isn't at all amusing being broke, — even in the

Chez Thomas Cook et fils
11 bis rue Cannebière
Marseille (B. du R.)
July 27, 1926

My dear Locke,

I am sorry that "because of your much abused candor in the past" you dropped corresponding with me also!

Well, if such stuff is the artistic temperament compost. I must be satisfied.

I'm staying here in Marseille which is the cheapest place in France for a man like myself without resources. Hope I shall have a chance of seeing you.

(left)
FIRST PAGE OF LETTER FROM LANGSTON HUGHES TO ALAIN LOCKE, MAY 4, 1926

After winning critical recognition, Hughes enrolled at Lincoln University in Pennsylvania and graduated in 1929. Shortage of funds was frequently a problem for Hughes during these student years. More than once, his breezy letters to Locke included an urgent request for a "ten."
MOORLAND-SPINGARN RESEARCH CENTER, HOWARD UNIVERSITY

(right)
LETTER FROM CLAUDE MCKAY TO ALAIN LOCKE, MARSEILLES, JULY 27, 1926

Judging from McKay's allusion here to Locke's "'much abused candor'" as a critic, the relationship between Locke and the Harlem writers was not always smooth. Elsewhere in this letter, McKay talked of Black critics' reaction to the sometimes harsh realism of his work. "Although I have strong racial opinions," he confided, "I cannot mix up art and racial propaganda. I must write what I feel ... and your Afro-American Intelligentsia won't like it."
MOORLAND-SPINGARN RESEARCH CENTER, HOWARD UNIVERSITY

COUNTÉE CULLEN
1903–1946

*"Yet I do marvel at this curious thing:/ To make a poet black and bid him sing."
With these words Countée Cullen voiced the irony of his position as a Black artist
in American society. One of the few Harlem artists to grow up there, Cullen began
writing poetry in high school, and his first major collection of poems—Color—
appeared when he was only twenty-two. Although his verse took the traditional
lyric form, his subject matter was drawn primarily from the contemporary Black
experience. Nevertheless, Cullen's viewpoint was not parochial. As one critic
observed, "the virtue of his work lies in his personal response to an experience
which, however conditioned by his race, is not so much racial as profoundly
human."*
WINOLD REISS, PASTEL ON ARTIST BOARD, CIRCA 1925, 30¹/₁₆″ × 21½″
NATIONAL PORTRAIT GALLERY, SMITHSONIAN INSTITUTION

PART II
The Decline of the Miraculous: Varying the Everyday Menu

In America the crude intractable facts of life, without which miracles never would have been necessary, were being dissolved. The regularities of nature, by which men knew that they were alive and were only human—the boundaries of seasons, of indoors and outdoors, of space and time, and the uniqueness of each passing moment—all these were being confused. The old tricks of the miracle maker, the witch, and the magician became commonplace. Foods were preserved out of season, water poured from bottomless indoor containers, men flew up into space and landed out of the sky, past events were conjured up again, the living images and resounding voices of the dead were made audible, and the present moment was packaged for future use. When man could accomplish miracles, he began to lose his sense of the miraculous. Americans who could no longer expect the usual were in danger of depriving themselves of the charms of the unexpected.

The flavor of life had once come from winter's cold, summer's heat, the special taste and color of each season's diet. The American Democracy of Times and Places meant making one place and one thing more like another, by bringing each under the control of man. The flavor of fresh meat would be tasted anywhere anytime, summer would have its ice, winter would have its warmth.

In the eighteenth century, when a monotonous diet marked the lower classes, variety of food was a delight, a dissipation, and a privilege of the wealthy. Patrick Henry accused Thomas Jefferson of an effete taste for "French Cookery." In the "Log Cabin and Hard Cider" campaign of 1840, the Whigs boasted that their candidate, William Henry Harrison, lived on wholesome "raw beef without salt," while his aristocratic opponent, President Martin Van Buren, was alleged to luxuriate in strawberries, raspberries, celery, and cauliflower. "Democratic" enthusiasm at first made a virtue of crude and tasteless food, and obsession with the delights of the palate was considered a symptom of Old World decadence.

But in the years after the Civil War—and encouraged by the wartime need to develop a technology that would feed a large army—old ways were improved, and new ways were found to prepare food and transport it in edible condition through long distances of space and time. The new techniques found for condensing milk and refrigerating meat in transit, and the development of new strains of fruits and vegetables better suited to long-distance transport made the diet more than ever before independent of the seasons.

The very size of the nation paradoxically encouraged the finding of new ways to make life more uniform in different regions and among different social classes. The rapid rise and growth of American cities, as much as anything else, spread the growing and eating of fresh fruits and vegetables over the United States. By the mid-twentieth century the perfecting of inexpensive household refrigerators made it possible for millions of Americans to keep in their kitchens a supply of food that was more varied than that of the wealthy aristocrats of an earlier age.

GAIL BORDEN'S VACUUM PAN FOR CONDENSING MILK, 1853

Borden's first two applications for a patent on his condensing pan were rejected on the ground that others had already succeeded in condensing milk using other methods. After he demonstrated that the vacuum process was crucial in preventing decomposition of the milk once it had been sealed in a can, officials finally recognized the originality of Borden's work and granted him a patent in 1856. DIVISION OF AGRICULTURE, THE NATIONAL MUSEUM OF HISTORY AND TECHNOLOGY, SMITHSONIAN INSTITUTION

112

GAIL BORDEN
1801–1874

Hearing of the food shortages experienced by the Forty-Niners on their trek westward, Texas landowner Gail Borden became fascinated with the possibility of reducing food to forms that were both easily transported and immune to spoilage. By 1850 he was manufacturing a dried meat biscuit which met these specifications. Although the biscuit venture proved a failure, Borden's interest in condensed food did not abate, and within five years he had developed a vacuum process for making condensed milk. It was not, however, until the Union Army made it a staple in the soldier's diet during the Civil War that Borden's concentrated milk finally became a commercial success.

G. MAYNARD, CRAYON ON PAPER, DATE UNKNOWN, 34″ × 29″ (SIGHT)
BORDEN, INC.

113

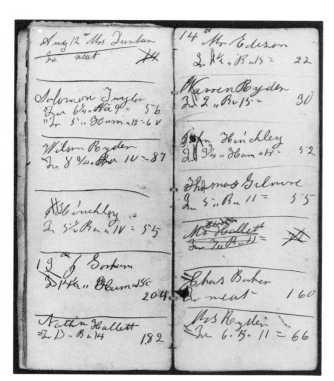

SWIFT'S ACCOUNT
BOOK,
1859–60

(left)
During his early days as a meat peddler in Barnstable, Massachusetts, Swift kept his accounts in this pocket-size notebook.
THE CHICAGO HISTORICAL SOCIETY

GUSTAVUS SWIFT
1839–1903

(right)
Before Gustavus Swift established his Chicago meat-packing house in 1875, providing distant markets with fresh beef and pork meant shipping animals on the hoof. In-transit feeding, however, and freight rates figured on the basis of total animal weight made this a costly proposition. Swift was determined to reduce these expenses. After winter experiments in shipping dressed meat in conventional freight cars brought increased profits, he commissioned the development of a refrigerator which would permit shipment of dressed carcasses throughout the year. By 1881 Swift was operating ten such cars between Chicago and Eastern markets. The following year, with other packers following suit and retail prices declining accordingly, Harper's Weekly *proclaimed the "era of cheap beef."*
RALPH CLARKSON, OIL ON CANVAS, 1904, 36" × 29"
NATIONAL PORTRAIT GALLERY, SMITHSONIAN INSTITUTION, GIFT OF GEORGE H. SWIFT, JR.

114

PHILIP DANFORTH
ARMOUR
1832–1901

Arriving in Chicago the same year as Swift, meat-packer Philip Danforth Armour shared his competitor's preoccupation with expanding markets and reducing expenses. By the 1890's, taking full advantage of advances in refrigeration, Armour and Company was supplying meat to markets throughout the world. More remarkable was Armour's genius for systematizing production and eliminating waste. As Chicago humorist "Mr. Dooley" put it, with but small exaggeration, "A cow goes lowin' softly into Armours an' comes out glue, gelatin, fertylizer, celooid, . . . hair restorer, washin' sody, . . . an bed springs so quick that while aft she's still a cow, for'ard she may be anything fr'm buttons to pannyma hats."
ARMOUR AND COMPANY

115

The Jungle
By Upton Sinclair

It was four o'clock when the ceremony was over and the carriages began to arrive. There had been a crowd following all the way, owing to the exuberance of Marija Berczynskas. The occasion rested heavily upon Marija's broad shoulders — it was her task to see that all things went in due form, and after the best home traditions; and, flying wildly hither and thither, bowling every one out of the way, and exhorting and scolding all day with her tremendous voice, Marija was too eager to see that others conformed to the proprieties to consider them herself. She had left the church last of all, and desiring to arrive first at the hall, had issued orders to the coachman to drive faster. When that personage had developed a will of his own in the matter, Marija had flung up the window of the carriage, and, leaning out, proceeded to tell him her

opinion of him, first in Lithuanian, which he did not understand, and then in Polish, which he did. Having the advantage of her in altitude, the driver had stood his ground and even ventured to attempt to speak; and the result had been a furious altercation, which, continuing all the way down Ashland Avenue, had added a new swarm of urchins to the cortege at each street for half a mile.

This was unfortunate, for already there was a throng before the door. The music had started up, and half a block away you could hear the dull "broom, broom" of the cello, with the squeaking of two fiddles which vied with each other in intricate and altitudinous gymnastics. Seeing the throng, Marija abandoned precipitely the debate concerning the ancestors of her coachman, and, springing from the moving carriage, plunged in and proceeded to clear a way to the hall. Once within, she turned and began to

MANUSCRIPT FRAGMENT OF *THE JUNGLE*

The Jungle opened innocently with scenes of a festive Lithuanian wedding in "Packingtown." But even the non-squeamish became both fascinated and disgusted, not only by detailed descriptions of the sights, sounds, and smells of the slaughterhouses, but also by revelations of condemned meat sold instead of destroyed, workers losing their hands in stamping machines and their lives in lard vats, spoiled meat doctored, canned, or made into sausage, and prepared meat that included filth, germs, and poisoned rats.
LILLY LIBRARY, INDIANA UNIVERSITY, BLOOMINGTON

116

UPTON SINCLAIR
1878-1968

"I aimed at the public's heart, and by accident I hit it in the stomach," said Upton Sinclair of the phenomenal success of his novel The Jungle *(1906). Intending to arouse sympathy for the immigrants working as "wage slaves" of the "Beef Trust" and living in Chicago's slums, the young socialist wrote instead a shocking exposé of the meat-packing industry. Americans could no longer take for granted the sanitariness or wholesomeness of what they ate. President Theodore Roosevelt, who remembered with distaste the canned meat provided for soldiers during the Spanish-American War, urged Congress to pass the Meat Inspection Act and the Pure Food and Drug Act (1906). Unconvinced, Sinclair remained a vegetarian.*

CARL J. ELDH, PLASTER, 1926, 24″ HIGH

LILLY LIBRARY, INDIANA UNIVERSITY, BLOOMINGTON

117

LORENZO DELMONICO 1813–1881

Nineteen-year-old Lorenzo Delmonico was not thinking of the hoi polloi *when he persuaded his uncles to open New York's first restaurant offering* haute cuisine *to the upper class. The Swiss immigrant's enterprise was an immediate success, attracting the desired clientele and becoming influential. Restaurants appeared all over America imitating Delmonico's; Parisian chefs came to New York hoping to work for him. Delmonico reformed the eating habits of all classes. By teaching Americans to eat salads, to use locally grown vegetables, and to prepare the abundant varieties of native fish and game, he proved their diet could be inexpensive without being monotonous or unhealthful.*

UNIDENTIFIED ARTIST, WOOD ENGRAVING, PUBLISHED AT THE TIME OF DELMONICO'S DEATH

MUSEUM OF THE CITY OF NEW YORK

A STAG DINNER AT DELMONICO'S, 1857

Delmonico transformed America's social behavior as well as its diet. The institution of the restaurant flourished as more Americans "dined out." The commercially and socially useful stag dinners at Delmonico's led to the formation of gentlemen's clubs. In the 1870's the lavishness of the catered coming-out parties, balls, and dinners given by the rich became notorious.
WOODCUT ENGRAVING IN *Harper's Weekly*, MAY 2, 1857
SMITHSONIAN INSTITUTION LIBRARIES

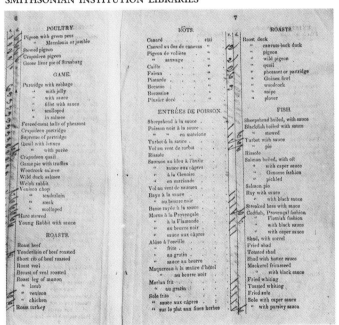

A SECTION OF DELMONICO'S ELEVEN-PAGE MENU, 1838

There ne'er was seen so fair a sight
As at Delmonico's last night;
When feathers, flowers, gems and lace
Adorned each lovely form and face;
A garden of all thorns bereft
The outside world behind them left . . .
     —Anonymous

Delmonico's elegant customers enjoyed attentive service in sumptuous surroundings among their peers. One of the restaurant's greatest attractions was its unique menu. Despite his success, Delmonico long continued to do his own marketing; he provided not only expensive imported delicacies but also a range of ingeniously prepared and tasty domestic fish, game, and vegetables.
MUSEUM OF THE CITY OF NEW YORK

119

LUTHER BURBANK
1849–1926

Luther Burbank, "the farmer's Edison," rationalized nature; the gentle Darwinian accelerated natural selection by thousands of years. Extraordinarily sensitive to plants, Burbank could choose the fittest among six hundred plum seedlings grafted onto a single tree. For fifty years he crossbred and selected among hundreds of thousands of varieties of plums, prunes, berries, potatoes, apples, peaches, quinces, nectarines, tomatoes, corn, squash, asparagus, peas, etc., to find the hardiest, easiest to grow and transport, tastiest, and most attractive. Burbank made fruit and vegetable farming more profitable and less chancy, ensuring fresh fruit and vegetables to Americans in every region, whatever the season.
FRED HARTSOOK, PHOTOGRAPH, 1915
LIBRARY OF CONGRESS

LUTHER BURBANK AMONG HIS POPPIES

Burbank's New Creations in Fruits and Flowers *(1893) triggered hostility that astonished him; he never doubted the truth in Darwin nor saw "blasphemy" in experimenting with nature. In 1926 another such torrent of venom, following Burbank's admission he was an "infidel," may have shortened his life. To the end he felt that "church sounds and smells are not as pleasing . . . as those of open, sunny fields of flowers."*
LIBRARY OF CONGRESS

121

**NATHANIEL JARVIS
WYETH
1802-1856**

The ice on New England's ponds in winter, like the grass on western prairies, was a natural resource free for the taking. An inventive harvester, Nathaniel J. Wyeth joined forces with an enterprising marketeer, Frederick Tudor, to make ice (once a luxury) into a household commonplace. Wyeth developed a horsepowered ice plow that rapidly and efficiently cut uniform blocks of ice; his implements for preserving, storing, and handling ice made shipment along the East Coast economical; and he built an export market which extended from Havana to Bombay. But Wyeth—who had invented nearly every device in use in the ice business at the time of his death—was never shrewd enough to make the fortune he sought.

UNIDENTIFIED ARTIST, WOOD ENGRAVING, PROBABLY AFTER A DAGUERREOTYPE OR EARLY PHOTOGRAPH

OREGON HISTORICAL SOCIETY

HAND-POWERED ICE
PLOW, WYETH
DESIGN

*During his childhood on Fresh Pond in Cambridge, Massachusetts, Wyeth must
often have seen the deep ruts horse-drawn sleighs made in ice. He adapted this
principle for hand- and horse-powered ice plows. The hand plow's gradated
notched blades would deepen the initial cut as the spaces between them allowed the
ice shavings to escape.*
DEPARTMENT OF SCIENCE AND TECHNOLOGY, THE NATIONAL MUSEUM OF HISTORY
AND TECHNOLOGY, SMITHSONIAN INSTITUTION

ICE CUTTING ON
ROCKLAND LAKE

*Long after mechanical refrigeration and ice making were technically feasible, the
harvesting of natural ice remained economical and profitable. Wyeth designed the
ice plows, horse-powered elevators, chutes, and storehouses shown in this
lithograph.*
G. AND W. ENDICOTT AFTER DRAWING BY JOHN W. HILL, LITHOGRAPH, CIRCA 1850
THE OLD PRINT SHOP, NEW YORK CITY

123

JACOB PERKINS
1766–1849

Jacob Perkins was best known for his engraving process which made the counterfeiting of bank notes nearly impossible. In other ways, too, he expressed his inventive imagination. In 1834 Perkins received the first American patent on a device for mechanical refrigeration. A closed-circuit system in which ether was cooled in a tank of cold water and then passed to a chamber where it made ice, his invention held great promise. Unfortunately, the lack of interest by investors soon forced Perkins to drop his plans for manufacturing it on a large scale.

A. KNEISEL LITHOGRAPH, 1833

NATIONAL PORTRAIT GALLERY, SMITHSONIAN INSTITUTION

JOHN GORRIE
1803–1855

(left)
Dr. John Gorrie became interested in mechanical refrigeration through his investigations into the causes and cures of malaria in Apalachicola, Florida. Convinced that the survival rate of malaria victims could be increased by reducing the atmospheric temperature, he devised a primitive air-conditioning system for Apalachicola's hospital rooms. The ice required by Gorrie's system, however, was an expensive and often rare commodity in Florida. By 1845 he had developed an ice maker which, when finally perfected, was capable of producing ice blocks the size of bricks. But Gorrie's invention, like that of Perkins before him, went unheralded; and it was not until many years after his death that the value of his work was finally recognized.
CHARLES ADRIAN PILLARS, MARBLE, 1914
NATIONAL STATUARY HALL COLLECTION, U.S. CAPITOL

PATENT MODEL OF
JOHN GORRIE'S ICE
MAKER

(right)
Gorrie's ice-making machine used air to absorb the heat of an "uncongealable gas." In its cooled state, the gas then passed around a container of water, which soon turned to ice. "By this arrangement," Gorrie explained, "I accomplish my object with the least possible expenditure of force, and produce artificial refrigeration in greater quantity from atmospheric air than can be done by any [other] known means."
DEPARTMENT OF SCIENCE AND TECHNOLOGY, THE NATIONAL MUSEUM OF HISTORY
AND TECHNOLOGY, SMITHSONIAN INSTITUTION

CLARENCE
BIRDSEYE
1886-1956

"My contribution was to take Eskimo knowledge and the scientists' theories and adapt them to quantity production," said Clarence Birdseye, who brought Americans fresh food out of season. Insatiably curious and inventive, Birdseye held three hundred patents. While fur trading in Labrador, he "saw natives catching fish in fifty below zero weather, which froze stiff almost as soon as they were taken out of the water. Months later, when they were thawed out, some of these fish were still alive." Birdseye's experiments resulted in a multiple-plate direct-contact freezer in which small packages of food were instantaneously frozen, leaving cell tissue, taste, and nutritional value intact. Birdseye became Birds Eye—meaning strawberries in December and seafood in Kansas.
GENERAL FOODS CORPORATION

126

PART III
A Popular Culture

There was no mystery about what gave Old World civilizations their aristocratic character. Culture and wealth were in the hands of a few, and just as earlier revolutions had aimed to open the vehicles and instruments of knowledge to larger numbers, Old World revolutions since the nineteenth century aimed to distribute property more widely to accomplish justice or equality. American civilization, in the course of fulfilling its democratic mission, would diffuse property and give it novel forms. The liberal movements of early modern times had brought knowledge out of the dusty recesses of Greek and Latin, Hebrew and Arabic, into the fresh air of the vernacular. In the United States the democratizing of language and knowledge went one bold step further. The colloquial language and what passed for knowledge in the marketplace became the arbiters of the classroom and the academy. Knowledge and the arts were redefined—and new institutions designed—to make them accessible and appealing.

FROM PACKING TO PACKAGING: A DEMOCRACY OF THINGS

In the United States by the early twentieth century, all sorts of objects were being offered in newly attractive garb—creating a democracy of things. In the Old World, even after the industrial age had arrived, only expensive items were housed in their own box or elegantly wrapped. A

127

watch or a jewel would be presented in a carefully fashioned container, but the notion that a pound of sugar or a dozen crackers should be encased and offered for purchase in specially designed, attractive materials seemed outlandish. Essential to the American Standard of Living were new techniques for clothing objects to make them appealing advertisements for themselves. Industries spent fortunes improving the sales garb of inexpensive objects of daily consumption—a pack of cigarettes or a can of soup.

Just as the rise of factory-made clothing and the new American democracy of clothing leveled people and made it increasingly difficult to distinguish a man's occupation, his bank account, or the status of his family by what he wore, so it was with packaging. Here was a new way of democratizing objects, of leveling and assimilating their appearance. By looking at a newly designed machine-made package, it was hard to tell the quality of the object inside, and sometimes hard to tell even what the object was.

By the mid-twentieth century, packaging (which had entered the lives of Americans unheralded and unchronicled) dominated the consciousness of the American consumer.

CHARLES HILL
MORGAN
1831–1911

Charles H. Morgan's innovation is now so commonplace as to seem a work of nature. As a machinist and draftsman for carpet manufacturer Erastus Bigelow, Morgan had made improvements in loom design and construction. In 1860 he turned his attention to paper bags and developed the first commercially feasible automatic machine to manufacture them. Although he and his brother sold their Philadelphia plant for a profit in 1864, Morgan's contribution to harried salesclerks and hurried shoppers remains essentially unchanged and utterly indispensable after a century.
PHOTOGRAPH, CIRCA 1900
MORGAN CONSTRUCTION COMPANY

**JAMES MCKEEN
CATTELL
1860–1944**

James M. Cattell's work and leadership helped transform psychology from a branch of philosophy into a social science. Objectifying the subjective was a goal Cattell brought closer by his "order-of-merit" method of testing developed in 1902. By using large numbers of subjects to correct for "wrong" answers, he could quantify qualitative judgments—such as the relative brightness of two hundred shades of gray—and "explain" the perception. With this help, manufacturers soon learned to use packaging scientifically to appeal to the greatest number of customers. In 1921 Cattell organized more than a hundred psychologists to form the Psychological Corporation, intended to provide business with practical applications of their research and theories.

BACHRACH PHOTOGRAPH, CIRCA 1925

DR. PSYCHE CATTELL

LEARNING FOR ALL

Never before had democracy been tried on such a large scale, nor allowed to shape the academic standards of a whole nation. Underlying the democratic transformations of the ways of judging and measuring was a faith in "the people," in their inherent spontaneous wisdom, in almost everybody's ability to learn almost anything, and a tendency to define "knowledge" as anything that anybody found useful.

In the United States, unlike the more settled countries of Western Europe, education became a curiously inverted pyramid. Institutions of "higher learning," presuming to offer the whole citizenry access to the most elevated and most difficult branches of learning, multiplied in numbers and without precedent—even before the nation had a suitably extensive and democratic apparatus of preparation. Higher learning spread over the land, in ambitious and pretentious institutions generously supported by public treasure, even before the courts of the states had removed doubts about whether it was legally permissible to collect taxes to support a public high school.

Democratizing the College: Land-Grant Colleges

Along with their prematurely grand hotels, nineteenth-century town-boosters built their own colleges and universities, ostensibly institutions of higher learning, each for his new Athens, his new Rome, or his new Oxford. The grandeur of these institutions lay in the future, and as often as not that future never came. By the mid-century, the United States was already being called "a land of colleges." But the mortality rate of colleges, as of towns, was high. There were ghost colleges to match the ghost towns. Before 1860, over seven hundred American colleges had died. Of the colleges and universities founded before the Civil War, fewer than one in five was still in operation by 1930.

A New Higher Education came into being in the United States after 1850. It was a product of many American circumstances. Curiously enough, it had been made possible by the very emptiness of the continent, which unexpectedly proved to be a main resource for building and supporting the new institutions. The lands owned by the federal government and held for all the American people were what made possible the land-grant colleges. While they were only one of many kinds of American institutions of higher education, they were a decisively new influence. For example, "coeducation" (an American word which first came into common use in the era of the land-grant colleges) was largely their by-product. It was appropriate, too, that the gospel of the New Higher Education should not come from the great Eastern cities, which lay in the shadow of Old World learning, but from the West.

The age of the land-grant college saw other acts of faith in the new religion of education. The earliest American private colleges—Harvard, Yale, Princeton, Dartmouth, Amherst—had been founded with relatively small capital sums, aided later by generous public grants and by the modest philanthropy of their loyal sons. Then the booster colleges before the Civil War had depended on the meager resources of the denominations or on piecemeal support from local communities. The years between the end of the Civil War and the beginning of World War I were an era of great private philanthropies.

The late years of the nineteenth century saw educational philanthropy on a new scale. With a few exceptions—Rockefeller was a high school graduate and Leland Stanford had attended an academy—the new cathedrals of higher learning were founded by self-made men who had little or no formal education themselves. Their munificence was rooted in faith—and in belief that a great democratic nation required numerous new kinds of institutions offering a newly democratized kind of learning. At the inauguration of Drexel Institute in 1891, Chauncey Depew, president of the New York Central Railroad, complained that the culture of the classical college had become "the veneer of the quack, and finally the decoration of the dude." "The old education," he said, "simply trained the mind. The new trains the mind, the muscles, and the sense. The old education gave the intellectual a vast mass of information useful in the library and useless in the shop."

There was nothing anywhere else quite like the array of American colleges or universities, or the speed with which they grew. In 1870 the United States had 563 institutions of higher learning. By 1910, when these institutions numbered nearly 1,000, their enrolled students totaled one third of a million. At that time the 16 universities of France enrolled altogether about forty thousand students, a number nearly equalled by the faculty members of the American institutions. By 1935, American institutions numbered some 1,500 with over one million students; by 1960 the institutions numbered 2,000 with over three million students. And by 1975 the institutions numbered nearly 3,000 with over ten million students.

JONATHAN
BALDWIN TURNER
1805–1899

How could Americans tolerate a college system devoted almost entirely to a "professional" class that comprised only 5 percent of the population? For Yale-trained classics professor Jonathan Baldwin Turner at Illinois College, the answer was a resounding they-could-not. With this, Turner began his crusade for the federally endowed, vocationally oriented state university. Although it was left to others to make his dream a reality, there was little doubt that Turner's many speaking and pamphlet campaigns helped substantially to build up the momentum which culminated in the passage of a federal college land-grant act in 1862.

PHOTOGRAPH, CIRCA 1868
ILLINOIS HISTORICAL SURVEY, UNIVERSITY OF ILLINOIS LIBRARY

132

JUSTIN S. MORRILL
1810–1898

(left)
Justin Morrill agreed with many of his contemporaries that traditional college subjects should be supplemented "by those of a less antique and more practical value." In 1857 he introduced legislation to support agricultural and mechanical education. Morrill's bill, which became law in 1862, gave each state thirty thousand acres of public land for each congressman. The proceeds from the sale of this land were to be invested and the income used to finance the new type of education.

The Morrill Land Grant Act had an immediate impact: it enabled older universities to introduce programs in the mechanical arts and provided new state universities dedicated to such programs with the funds necessary for their survival.
PRESTON POWERS, MARBLE, 1875, 28″ HIGH
ON INDEFINITE LOAN TO THE NATIONAL PORTRAIT GALLERY FROM THE NATIONAL COLLECTION OF FINE ARTS, SMITHSONIAN INSTITUTION

(right)
Letter from Justin Morrill to Jonathan Baldwin Turner thanking Turner for his perseverance in the land-grant cause, December 30, 1861
ILLINOIS HISTORICAL SURVEY, UNIVERSITY OF ILLINOIS LIBRARY

JOHNS HOPKINS
1794–1873

Johns Hopkins' gift of $7 million to found a hospital and university set a standard for educational benefaction which few later philanthropists could match. Hopkins, who amassed his fortune as a merchant, banker, and railroad executive, held no particular educational philosophy and provided no directions for the university's curriculum. His will included specific instructions, however, for the establishment of a medical school to cooperate with the hospital.

Hopkins' philanthropy surprised many of his contemporaries. They knew him as a private, unostentatious man who had never married and who had devoted all his energy to making money. There is no doubt, however, that he considered his gift the capstone of his career.

ALFRED JACOB MILLER, OIL ON CANVAS, CIRCA 1835, 30″ × 25″
THE JOHNS HOPKINS UNIVERSITY

134

ANDREW CARNEGIE
1835-1919

The individual who amasses great wealth, declared Pittsburgh steelmaker Andrew Carnegie in his Gospel of Wealth *in 1889, must in the end apply his fortune for the benefit of all. The possessor of one of the world's largest fortunes, Carnegie took his mandate seriously. By the time of his death he had turned over a staggering $350 million for benevolent purposes. Carnegie's unprecedented largesse was matched only by its social impact. His Teachers Pension Fund raised instructional standards in colleges; his many library endowments provided Americans with a national system of public libraries; and the Carnegie Corporation, established in 1911, became the prototype for the great philanthropic foundations of the modern day.*

UNIDENTIFIED ARTIST, OIL ON CANVAS, DATE UNKNOWN, 50″ × 40″
NATIONAL PORTRAIT GALLERY, SMITHSONIAN INSTITUTION, GIFT OF MRS.
MARGARET CARNEGIE MILLER

CARICATURE OF
ANDREW CARNEGIE,
LIFE, APRIL 13, 1905

Cartoons depicting his philanthropies as haphazard notwithstanding, Carnegie liked to believe that his giving was based on the systematic scheme set forth in The Gospel of Wealth. *In fulfilling his obligation to turn over his wealth for public uses, he declared, the man of fortune should view his task "scientifically." In Carnegie's philanthropic lexicon, this meant that outright gifts to poor individuals were less desirable than institutional endowments which promised to benefit large numbers for many generations. He further advised his fellow millionaires that certain enterprises were more worthy than others. While universities stood foremost in his listing of desirable philanthropies, much to the dismay of clergymen, churches ranked last.*

NATIONAL PORTRAIT GALLERY, SMITHSONIAN INSTITUTION

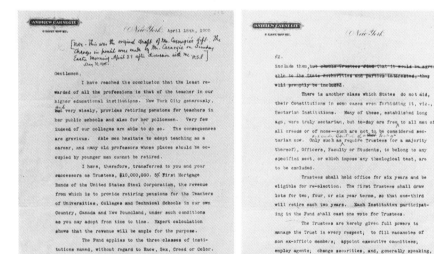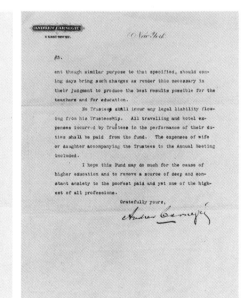

DRAFT OF LETTER
ESTABLISHING
TEACHERS PENSION
FUND, APRIL 18, 1905

Because it required that participating schools drop their sectarian affiliations and meet certain academic standards, Carnegie's Teachers Pension Fund had an impact on American higher education far beyond its immediate goal of providing college teachers with a comfortable retirement income.

THE CARNEGIE FOUNDATION FOR THE ADVANCEMENT OF TEACHING, NEW YORK

136

LELAND STANFORD
1824–1893

Wanting to raise a memorial to his recently deceased son, Leland Stanford decided that the most fitting tribute would be a university. In 1885, endowed with his gift of $5 million, Leland Stanford Junior University came into existence. As builder of the Central Pacific Railroad—which, when united with the Union Pacific in 1869, formed the nation's first transcontinental railroad—Stanford knew at first hand the scarcity of professionally trained engineers. With this in mind, he urged that the new university stress training in the practical sciences. Equally important to Stanford was its accessibility. Until his death in 1893, he took special care that the school's fees remain within easy reach of poor students.

JEAN LOUIS MEISSONIER, OIL ON CANVAS, 1881, 40″ × 32″

STANFORD UNIVERSITY MUSEUM OF ART, STANFORD FAMILY COLLECTION

LELAND STANFORD
SURVEYING HIS
NEWLY
ESTABLISHED
UNIVERSITY

(left)
The caption accompanying this cartoon read: "It is all for you my boy, and for the coming generations. My ambition is now satisfied. I have less desire to be President than to be founder of an institution that will make Presidents!" These were almost prophetic words, considering that Herbert Hoover was a member of Stanford University's first graduating class.
CARTOON CUT FROM *Wasp,* DATE UNKNOWN
STANFORD UNIVERSITY ARCHIVES

(right)
Featured on the elaborately decorated speakers' platform was a full-length portrait of the Stanfords' dead son, in whose memory the university had been created.
STANFORD UNIVERSITY ARCHIVES

MR. AND MRS.
LELAND STANFORD
SEATED ON THE
PLATFORM AT THE
DEDICATION OF
STANFORD
UNIVERSITY,
OCTOBER 1, 1891

MATTHEW VASSAR
1792–1868

In the 1850's, it was still widely believed that, being the "weaker vessel," woman could not survive the rigors of higher education. Thanks largely to the influence of a principal from a neighboring girls' seminary, Vassar, a brewer from Poughkeepsie, New York, did not agree. In 1861, determined to dedicate his fortune to "some charitable purpose," he established a fund for a college devoted to the education of women. Four years later Vassar Female College opened its doors with a capacity enrollment. While many labeled it "Vassar's Folly," the founder considered the school his greatest achievement. In his diary in 1864, comparing himself to Lincoln, Vassar wrote: "Two Noble Emancipists—one of women—[the other of] the Negro."

CHARLES LORING ELLIOTT, OIL ON CANVAS, 1861, 96″ × 63″
VASSAR COLLEGE ART GALLERY

139

JAMES B. DUKE
1856–1925

"I recognize that education, when conducted along sane and practical . . . lines, is, next to religion, the greatest civilizing influence," wrote James Buchanan Duke when he signed the indenture creating a $40 million trust fund in 1924. Chief beneficiary of his philanthropy was Duke University, formerly Trinity College and now one of the nation's best-endowed educational institutions.

Duke had made his fortune in the tobacco and electric-power businesses, but he suggested that the university curriculum concentrate on training teachers, preachers, lawyers, and physicians. In his opinion, *"These are most in the public eye, and by precept and example can do most to uplift mankind . . ."*

JOHN DA COSTA, OIL ON CANVAS, DATE UNKNOWN, 50″ × 40″ (SIGHT)
DUKE UNIVERSITY

CONSTRUCTION OF
WEST CAMPUS,
DUKE UNIVERSITY,
MAY 1930

DUKE UNIVERSITY ARCHIVES

The Rise of the High School

To prepare student minds (as well as student bodies) for a truly "higher" education, there would have to be preparatory institutions above the elementary grade open to all citizens. The obvious answer to this need was the "high school." The expression itself was an Americanism which had appeared earlier in the nineteenth century to describe any school beyond the elementary level where students were taught "all those branches which fit a young man for college."

To complete a democratic apparatus of education, these high schools would have to become universal, free, and public. Never before in any modern nation had there been such a need, simply because the opportunity to enter institutions of higher learning had never been so widespread. The free public high school, which would prove one of the nation's most significant, most distinctive, and least celebrated institutions, was an American invention.

For all practical purposes, the American high school was a creature of the twentieth century. Not until 1874 did the classic statement by Chief Justice Thomas M. Cooley of the Michigan Supreme Court finally dissolve doubts of the legality of the tax-supported public high school. As late as 1890, the high school had touched only a tiny minority of the American people; of the nation's children aged fourteen to seventeen years, the number enrolled in all high schools and private secondary schools amounted to less than 7 percent. Of that number, only an insignificant percentage went on to college. In 1897, when President

141

Charles W. Eliot of Harvard described "the function of education in a democratic society," he was announcing a hope and not recording a fact. "Democratic education being a very new thing in the world," he explained, "its attainable objects are not yet fully perceived."

By 1920 the proportion of the high-school-age population attending high school had reached one-third, by 1950 the figure was three-quarters and every year going up, until by 1970 the number was nearly 90 percent. The new American religion of education was becoming universal, and the high school was every citizen's place of worship.

CHARLES W. ELIOT
1834–1926

Appointed president of Harvard in 1869, Charles W. Eliot believed that the nation's colleges must attract students from a broader social spectrum. This, however, required substantial upgrading in secondary schools. By the 1880's, while overseeing Harvard's most ambitious expansion program, Eliot was actively urging the reform of lower schools. As chairman of the National Education Association's "Committee of Ten" in 1892, he outlined proposals for a much-enriched secondary curriculum designed to prepare and encourage students to seek college training. Criticized for ignoring the need for vocational education, the Committee's report nevertheless inspired many changes in the high school and, along with Eliot's other efforts, spread the belief that college should no longer be a preserve for the privileged few.

ANNIE WARE SABINE-SIEBERT, WATERCOLOR ON IVORY, 1923, 5″ × 3¾″
NATIONAL PORTRAIT GALLERY, SMITHSONIAN INSTITUTION, GIFT OF ELIZABETH L. HOWIE AND JOHN F. MARSHALL

JOHN DEWEY
1859–1952

In establishing the Laboratory School at the University of Chicago in 1896, John Dewey intended to provide primary and secondary students with a new type of education. Instead of teaching students through the rote methods used in most schools, he made his classrooms laboratories of real-life experience. There, by doing, students would learn to adapt their beliefs and skills to new experiences. Dewey's experiment was not without critics. Although traditionalists described his school as a "riot of uncontrolled liberty," Dewey's influence spread as schools across the country hastened to incorporate his methods into their curriculum.

JOSEPH MARGULIES, WATERCOLOR ON PAPER, CIRCA 1946, 14″ × 11″
NATIONAL PORTRAIT GALLERY, SMITHSONIAN INSTITUTION

143

PHOTOGRAPHS OF
DEWEY'S
LABORATORY
SCHOOL

Lab School students and teachers planting a garden
A lesson in French
Learning to make wool

The curriculum at Dewey's Lab School embraced a wide range of activities. While foreign-language students perfected their skills in mealtime conversations, others were learning the physical properties of wool and elements of design by weaving fabrics. Young students received their first lessons in botany by observing the progress of the seeds they planted.
THE UNIVERSITY OF CHICAGO ARCHIVES

144

THE SCHOOL AND SOCIETY, BY JOHN DEWEY (1899)

The School and Society *was Dewey's comprehensive explanation of what he was trying to achieve at the "Lab" School. When the learning process was based on first-hand experience rather than memorization of abstract principles, the educator argued, it developed not only the child's intellectual ability but his imaginative, creative, and social capacities as well.*

THE UNIVERSITY OF CHICAGO ARCHIVES

145

HORACE MANN
1796–1859

As first Secretary of the Massachusetts State Board of Education from 1837 to 1849, Mann's annual reports and educational conventions served to inform and arouse public opinion in that state and nationally. Normal schools were established, modern methods of instruction introduced, and teacher salaries raised; the minimum school year was extended, $2 million spent on better schoolhouses and equipment, and fifty high schools built.

DAGUERREOTYPE MADE APRIL 5, 1858 AT ANTIOCH COLLEGE, YELLOW SPRINGS, OHIO

MASSACHUSETTS HISTORICAL SOCIETY

146

Culture for All

One of the beautiful ironies of modern American history was that the children of refugees from the Old World had the wealth, the leisure, and the technical means to return for a holiday to the scenes of their parents' poverty and oppression. There were few more vivid symbols of American democracy, or of the special relation of Americans to the world, than this reverse Odyssey of American tourists. The man whose ancestor had fled penniless and in desperation from Sicily or Ireland or Germany returned in comfort to rediscover the "romance" of the Old World.

In the last decades of the nineteenth century, Americans of wealth sent back to the United States millions of dollars' worth of painting and sculpture. Banker J. P. Morgan, sugar magnate Henry Havemeyer and his wife, Boston's flamboyant Isabella Gardner, and Chicago *grande dame* Mrs. Potter Palmer were but a few of the many Americans who eagerly culled Europe's capitals for Old World art. Sometimes haphazardly, sometimes with design, they purchased works of art in unequaled quantities. Their princely collections eventually became the nuclei of the many art museums which sprang into existence in the last quarter of the nineteenth century. Fine art, once the preserve of a select few, became an experience accessible to all.

CASSATT'S MURAL, *MODERN WOMAN,* FOR THE WOMAN'S BUILDING AT THE WORLD'S COLUMBIAN EXPOSITION, 1893

This building was entirely the work of women. Its organizer, Mrs. Palmer, commissioned Mary Cassatt to paint one of its murals. Cassatt's feminism, like Palmer's, was firm but not radical, as the center panel—"Young women plucking the fruits of Knowledge and Science"—shows. Murals were not Cassatt's métier, so it is perhaps fortunate for her reputation that this effort was displayed on a ceiling forty-eight feet high.
REPRODUCED IN *Art and Handicraft in the Woman's Building,* THE OFFICIAL HANDBOOK
SMITHSONIAN INSTITUTION LIBRARIES

MARY CASSATT   *Mary Cassatt, a brilliant American painter living abroad, joined the avant-garde*
1845-1926   *French impressionists in the 1870's, but stayed aloof from their bohemianism.*
Cassatt's respectable family and conventional life style led socially prominent art
buyers like Mrs. Potter Palmer and the insatiable Henry and Louisine Havemeyer
to seek her counsel. The works of artists little known in America and not yet
fashionable in Europe—of Cassatt herself, her friend and mentor Degas, Manet,
Renoir and others—as well as the neglected Spanish masters El Greco and Goya,
ultimately became public treasures via private legacies, such as the Havemeyers'
enormous gifts to the Metropolitan Museum of Art and Mrs. Palmer's gift to the
Art Institute of Chicago.
SELF-PORTRAIT, WATERCOLOR, CIRCA 1900, 13″ × 9½″
A. P. BERSOHN

148

BERTHA HONORÉ
PALMER
1849-1918

"An innkeeper's wife," snorted the Infanta Eulalia of Spain when snubbing *Chicago's leading socialite in 1893. No description of Mrs. Potter Palmer could have been less adequate, for few women in the late nineteenth century made better use of their social position.*

Her astute patronage hastened America's acceptance of the paintings of Mary Cassatt and other impressionist artists. She organized the Woman's Building at the World's Columbian Exposition and made it an effective, though limited, statement on women's abilities in all fields of endeavor. In addition to her social abilities, she possessed a business acumen that enabled her to double her husband's estate after his death in 1902.

ANDERS ZORN, ETCHING, 1896, 9⅜″ × 6¼″

NATIONAL PORTRAIT GALLERY, SMITHSONIAN INSTITUTION

149

LETTER FROM
MARY CASSATT TO
MRS. PALMER
ABOUT HER MURAL,
MODERN WOMAN

Mrs. Palmer faced her colleagues with a fait accompli *when she chose a "modern" painter for the Woman's Building, explaining that "Miss Cassatt had to build an immense glass-roofed building at her summer home, where, rather than work on a ladder, she arranged to have the canvas lowered into an excavation in the ground when she wished to work on the upper part of its surface." In this letter, dated October 11, 1892, Mary Cassatt described her mural and expressed some of the bitterness that poisoned her later life.*
THE ART INSTITUTE OF CHICAGO

SEARCH FOR NOVELTY:
THE SOCIAL INVENTOR

Americans organized in search of novelty, they democratized novelty, until they would finally make it commonplace. All the resources which had been used to lay tracks across the continent, to develop an American System of Manufacturing in its several versions, now went into American Systems of Inventing. In modern America, everything became an incentive for invention.

Then the momentum of production itself became an unexpected force toward innovation. The American System of Manufacturing, the American System of Advertising and of Distribution, the production of millions of similar objects, the democratized consumption of costly novelties, produced a need for slightly *dis*similar objects. The Annual Model came from a need to keep people buying, as well as from a relentless search for novel products. Next year's model had to be just different enough. This relentless search produced countless unexpected novelties—"solutions" to still undiscovered problems. American ingenuity and imagination would be challenged to find uses for these novelties and to persuade the American consumer that they were worth spending money on. Flow-technology, an assembly-line society, implied in itself the need, with scheduled regularity, to change, however slightly, the product that was flowing. But how different was different enough?

The process of invention was itself democratized and transformed. Of course there would still be the lonely inventor in his attic, obsessed by his bizarre private vision. But now, too, there was the Social Inventor. If not a species peculiar to America, he developed and flourished here and found this nation a congenial habitat. The new inventor was a Social Inventor in several ways.

He might be, like Thomas Edison, an Inventor-for-the-Market, who saw a widespread need and tried to satisfy it. This required an ability to imagine needs that people were not yet even aware of, an intuition of what the society was ready for, and a versatile capacity to adapt a new product to the newly complex machinery of production, advertising, and distribution. Edison, and others like him or following his example, organized their invention factories, an American institution to fulfill distinctively American possibilities.

Or the Social Inventor might be a member of one of the many new Communities of Inventors. Their incentives did not stem from any specific need of the market but from the autonomous needs of invention itself. They lived by the internal logic of novelty. For them each new thing required another. Finding the use or the market would be somebody else's problem. Working in islands freed from the everyday necessities of making a living by marketing their product, they had the power to require society to recast its needs to make their discoveries useful. They delighted in making silk purses out of sows' ears, for they were free to think of the neglected obvious and the feasible that still seemed outlandish. They produced solutions in search of problems.

Research and Development was the new American name for the purposes of these newly burgeoning American institutions. This concept did not become a focus of national interest until long after it had become a national institution. In the mid-twentieth century, when the nation had taken unprecedented leaps toward the democratization of higher learning, people still worried over the problems of schools and universities, but the nation as a whole seemed barely aware of the decisive and growing role of the industrial research laboratory.

Not until the Depression of the 1930's had stirred awareness of the connection between scientific progress, employment, and prosperity did statistics on such research become generally available. World War II was, of course, a potent incentive to Research and Development, and the pace increased during the postwar years. By 1956 the total national annual expenditure for Research and Development in the natural sciences alone came to nearly $8.5 billion, more than twice the total national expenditure in that year for all institutions of higher education. By the 1960's, "R&D" had entered dictionaries as another Americanism. Despite the dramatic increase of national expenditures on higher education (from some $7 billion in 1960 to $13 billion in 1965 and $23 billion in 1970), the growing annual expenditures on R&D remained steadily ahead, totaling $27 billion by 1970. While federal funds for this purpose were an ever-increasing proportion, the expenditures by private industrial firms, at least until the mid-twentieth century, accounted for fully half the totals.

But the industrial research laboratory was organized to seek in a new spirit. The men who searched in these laboratories were a new breed. It would be hard to make them popular heroes because they were working on frontiers that most Americans did not even know were there. They were no longer amateurs, nor rule-of-thumb men. They were no longer workers-in-attics, but scientist-statesmen with advanced training, using an esoteric language in the highest councils of the nation. No longer looking for some particular thing, they were going as much to seek as to find. The community emphasis, the vague hopes and booster optimisms of the earlier movers across physical America—they were now reliving all this in the mysterious wilderness of science. Not only legislation or the wisdom of statesmen but something else and something new was now shaping the American future. And of all things on earth, the growth of knowledge remained still the most spontaneous and unpredictable.

WILLIS R. WHITNEY
1868–1958

In 1901 General Electric hired Willis R. Whitney to direct the company's new industrial research laboratory. Whitney, a Massachusetts Institute of Technology chemistry professor who had developed a process making photographic film commercially practicable, shared General Electric's belief that "large industrial organizations have both an opportunity and a responsibility for their own life insurance. New discovery can provide it."

Under Whitney's leadership, General Electric's "House of Magic" encouraged such eminent scientists as Charles Steinmetz, Irving Langmuir, and William Coolidge to conduct research without consideration for its commercial applicability. Their discoveries in the electrical sciences, however, inevitably led to profit for General Electric and fame for the laboratory and its members.

PHOTOGRAPH IN *General Electric Review*, VOL. 36, NO. 1, JANUARY 1933
REPRODUCED WITH PERMISSION

IRVING LANGMUIR
1881–1957

Irving Langmuir combined pure and applied research during his career at the General Electric Research Laboratory. His work on the nature of gases, for example, produced a light bulb so efficient that, once in general use, it saved $1 million of electricity a day. An atomic hydrogen welding torch and high-vacuum radio tube were products of similarly open-ended experiments.

At the same time that Langmuir was making discoveries with direct commercial applicability, he won a 1932 Nobel Prize for his theoretical research in chemistry. This award, the first to an industrial scientist, signaled the bringing together of science and technology in the nation's new industrial research laboratories.

GENERAL ELECTRIC PHOTOGRAPH

DIVISION OF ELECTRICITY AND NUCLEAR ENERGY, THE NATIONAL MUSEUM OF
HISTORY AND TECHNOLOGY, SMITHSONIAN INSTITUTION

IRVING LANGMUIR
AND GUGLIELMO
MARCONI IN THE
GENERAL ELECTRIC
RESEARCH
LABORATORY

In 1920 Irving Langmuir escorted Guglielmo Marconi, the inventor of the wireless, through the General Electric Research Laboratory, where this photograph was taken. Langmuir's contribution to the development of the radio, while not as basic as Marconi's, was epochal: more than half of his sixty-five patents were concerned with radio engineering.

GENERAL ELECTRIC PHOTOGRAPH

DIVISION OF ELECTRICITY AND NUCLEAR ENERGY, THE NATIONAL MUSEUM OF HISTORY AND TECHNOLOGY, SMITHSONIAN INSTITUTION

155

GEORGE EASTMAN
1854–1932

George Eastman, a young Rochester, New York, bank teller, saw that taking pictures was an expensive, difficult, and cumbersome operation, even for highly skilled photographers. Eastman worked to simplify photography so that anyone who could aim and snap the camera and mail the film to his plant would receive finished pictures in return. From laboratories modeled on his friend Thomas Edison's Menlo Park, Eastman's scientists and engineers produced a steady stream of inventions that for a while gave him a near-monopoly of the domestic and international photographic industry. Reorganized as Kodak Research Laboratories in 1912, Eastman's was among the early corporate invention factories.

In 1876, when Eastman spent three weeks' salary ($94) on photographic equipment, he needed camera, lenses, glass plates, tripod, tent, chemicals, and assorted paraphernalia before he could take a single picture. Fourteen years later, like millions after him, he could go abroad with a black box in a shoulder bag and return with a lasting record of his experiences without writing a word, drawing a line, or dipping a single glass plate in emulsion.

Eastman is shown aboard ship en route to England in early 1890. The photograph was probably taken by his patent lawyer Fred Church. Eastman is holding what seems to be a Kodak No. 2 camera.

INTERNATIONAL MUSEUM OF PHOTOGRAPHY, ROCHESTER, NEW YORK

156

KODAK NO. 2   INTERNATIONAL MUSEUM OF PHOTOGRAPHY, ROCHESTER, NEW YORK
CAMERA

ARTHUR D. LITTLE
1863-1935

In 1921 Arthur D. Little made a silk purse out of sows' ears because he hated clichés about technology. A chemical engineer, Little specialized initially in paper and fiber technology, but branched out until his consultancy firm was reorganized in 1909 as Arthur D. Little, Inc., the biggest independent commercial research laboratory serving American industry. "Research," wrote Little, "is the mother of industry"—an assertion proven by his work in cellulose, petrochemicals, filtration, and other areas. Little had always had literary and philosophical leanings; "Little's Research Palace," willed on his death to the Massachusetts Institute of Technology, remained a "think tank" with a social dimension.

MARGARET FITZHUGH BROWNE, OIL ON CANVAS, 1939, 40″ × 34″

ARTHUR D. LITTLE, INC.

LITTLE'S SILK PURSE MADE FROM SOWS' EARS, 1921

From ten pounds of gelatine "manufactured wholly from sows' ears" Little spun an artificial silk thread, wove the thread into a fabric, and from the fabric made an elegant purse "of which both Her Serene and Royal Highness the Queen of the Burgundians in her palace, and the lowly Sukie in her sty, might well have been proud." But might not the same remarkable technology which defied folk wisdom also destroy our sense of wonder? "New impressions so crowd upon us," wrote Little, "that the miracle of yesterday is the commonplace of today."
DIVISION OF PHYSICAL SCIENCES, THE NATIONAL MUSEUM OF HISTORY AND TECHNOLOGY, SMITHSONIAN INSTITUTION

About the Author

DANIEL J. BOORSTIN, senior historian of the Smithsonian Institution in Washington, D.C., was the director of The National Museum of History and Technology from 1969 to 1973. Before that, he was Preston and Sterling Morton Distinguished Service Professor at the University of Chicago, where he taught on the history faculty for twenty-five years.

Born in Georgia in 1914 and raised in Tulsa, Oklahoma, he received his undergraduate degree with highest honors from Harvard University and his doctorate from Yale. As a Rhodes Scholar at Balliol College, Oxford, he won a coveted "double first" and was admitted as a barrister-at-law of the Inner Temple, London. More recently he has been visiting professor at the University of Rome, at Kyoto University, at the Sorbonne, and at Cambridge University, England, which awarded him its D.Litt. degree. He has lectured on American history widely within this country and all over the world. Dr. Boorstin is married to the former Ruth Frankel and has three sons.

Dr. Boorstin, whose works in American history, politics, law, and society have been translated into many languages, is editor of the thirty-two-volume *Chicago History of American Civilization*. Among his works are *The Lost World of Thomas Jefferson, The Genius of American Politics, The Image: A Guide to Pseudo-Events in America,* and *Democracy and Its Discontents.* His most extensive work is the trilogy *The Americans,* the three volumes of which were awarded the Bancroft, Parkman and Pulitzer prizes.